Praise for Evolved Assistant

This book encapsulates the essence of what every administrative professional, regardless of tenure or career stage, should strive to embody, display, and demand in their quest to deliver results in this critical role.

-BILL CONNORS, PRESIDENT, XFINITY

Tara's exceptional assistant career is reason enough to listen to her engaging and practical wisdom, but the intentionality and thoughtfulness woven throughout the Evolved Assistant makes it a must read for Leader Assistants of the world.

- JEREMY BURROWS, BESTSELLING AUTHOR OF THE LEADER ASSISTANT AND HOST OF THE LEADER ASSISTANT PODCAST

Feeling like there's a higher summit to reach? Like you've got mountains of potential still untouched? Spoiler alert: you do. I was right there with you. Then, Tara Sims' 'Evolved Assistant' happened. Most books stop at the 'what' and 'why', but Tara masterfully ventures into the HOW, delivering deep, thought-provoking inquiries and steps that aren't just theories, but actions to implement now. This isn't just another book—it's a wake up call for your potential. Don't ignore it. Your future is waiting, and it relies heavily on one thing: YOU. Dedicate the time, do the work, soak in the insights, and watch as you become the Evolved Assistant the world needs. Excellence is about to get a new definition.

-MAGGIE JACOBS, AUTHOR OF THE ELEVATED EA

I believe this book could literally be the roadmap for any administrative professional who wants to be valued, recognized, and who aspires to greatness in their career. The evolution of the administrative vocation is happening right now, and Evolved Assistant, with its thought-provoking strategies, ideas and exercises, will give you the tools you need to transform from being good to becoming exceptional in this career!

-DEBBIE GROSS, AUTHOR OF THE OFFICE ROCKSTAR PLAYBOOK

Tara Sims is someone who has walked the talk. Been there, done that, and got the t-shirt and some of the bumps along the way. This book is an important contribution to the conversation in the post pandemic world that we must have in order to move the profession forward.

-BONNIE LOW-KRAMEN, AUTHOR OF BE THE ULTIMATE ASSISTANT & STAFF MATTERS

FOREWORD BY BILL CONNORS, PRESIDENT, XFINITY

EVOLVED ASSISTANT

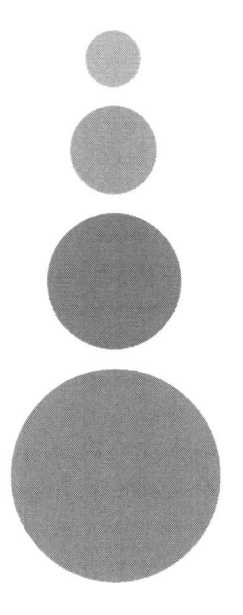

UNLOCKING SUCCESS IN A NEW ERA
FOR ADMINISTRATIVE PROFESSIONALS

TARA M SIMS

Evolved Assistant by Tara M Sims

Get your copy and learn more at www.evolvedassistant.com

Copyright © 2024 by Tara M Sims
All rights reserved.

All rights reserved. No part of this publication may be reproduced, distributed, or transmitted in any form or by any means, including photocopying, recording, or other electronic or mechanical methods, without the prior written permission of the publisher, except in the case of brief quotations embodied in critical reviews and certain other noncommercial uses permitted by copyright law. For permission requests, contact the author.

Publisher's Note

The information provided in this book is for general informational purposes only. While the author has made every effort to ensure the accuracy of the information herein, the publisher and author assume no responsibility for errors or omissions, or for damages that may result from the use of the information in this book.

Cover Design by Darnell McAlpin

Contents

Dedication	1
Foreword	3
By Bill Connors	
Preface	5
Definition	9
Introduction	11
Why Evolve	33
What Is An Evolved Assistant	49
Mindset	63
Growth vs. Fixed	
Confidence	
Strategic Partnership	
Organizational Priorities	
Systems	
Ownership vs. Employee	
Concierge Approach	
Management	121
Project Management	
A Sharper Toolkit	

    Time and Calendar Management
    Stealth-Like Behavior
    Boundaries

Marketing   151
    Personal Brand
    Personal Board of Directors
    Build Relationships
    Carve Your Career Path
    Challenging Office Culture

Maintenance   179
    Discretionary Effort
    Become Indispensable
    Experience Flow

Beyond Maintenance   193
    Intentionality
    Negativity
    Recognize Your Genius

Conclusion   209

Acknowledgments   213

Resources   217

References   221

About the author   223

This book is dedicated to the women who raised me to be strong, confident, and grateful:

Rosalind, Mildred, Margarite, Diane, Sharon.

Energy shifters, you taught me how to walk into a room and make a statement without saying a word.

I love you.

Foreword
By Bill Connors

When Tara approached me to write a foreword for her book, I experienced a momentary pause. This hesitation wasn't rooted in any reluctance to support her endeavors–in fact, I'm wholeheartedly behind anything she pursues. Rather, my brief pause stemmed from the awe I felt that Tara had actually written a book. It's a testament to her character–the boldness that defines how she thinks and engages with her work. I believe that same boldness is part of the spirit of this book that celebrates and helps guide all administrative professionals to think big and bold about how they approach their career journey.

Meeting Tara for the first time reminded me of my personal connection with the Executive Assistant role. My mother, Dorothy Connors, devoted over four decades to this profession across various companies and industries. From childhood, I absorbed firsthand accounts of my mother's work experiences through our nightly family dinners. Listening to my mom's stories made it evident to me that she was a driving force behind many companies' successes, even when she worked in roles where her manager didn't fully appreciate her contributions.

During that first meeting, when Tara interviewed for a position as my executive assistant, she made it clear that she wanted to lead and evolve. For Tara, a successful work partnership means being in an environment where her work is valued, and she is not just allowed–but encouraged–to be a key contributor. No matter the task, Tara understands that her work is essential to the organization. It is, and has always been, about far more than getting coffee and copying reports.

In *Evolved Assistant: Unlocking Success in a New Era for Administrative Professionals*, Tara unveils transformative principles that will empower you to unlock the secret to genuine success in your role, irrespective of the circumstances that may surround you. This book is a testament to Tara's journey and her commitment to empowering administrative professionals. Through her own experiences and those of others, she shares wisdom and insights to inspire and uplift you on your own path to success.

This book encapsulates the essence of what every administrative professional, regardless of tenure or career stage, should strive to embody, display, and demand in their quest to deliver results in this critical role. I encourage you to immerse yourself in Tara's book and find your way to making that bold, aspirational career happen. Here's to embracing evolution and the incredible journey that lies ahead for each of you!

Bill Connors
President, Xfinity

Preface

During those early months of the Covid-19 pandemic, so much uncertainty infiltrated every aspect of life. I, like so many others, found myself grappling with a profound sense of unease. The world around me was changing at a relentless pace, and I couldn't help but wonder where my own path would lead.

I have always been someone who, in times of uncertainty, takes the time to prepare for the unknown. I know you're probably thinking, "Um...Tara, how can you prepare for the unknown?" But it's my approach to the old saying, "Stay ready so you don't have to get ready," that always kicks in when life disruptions occur.

During this period of heightened introspection, a seed of realization took root within me. I thought, what if my boss, the one I had faithfully supported for years, decided he was now ready to retire? He was certainly able to make that decision, and, quite frankly, with all the intensity that the pandemic brought to our business, the largest American multinational telecommunications, and media conglomerate, it would not have completely shocked me if he had decided to announce, "I'm out of here." The mere thought gave me anxiety, triggering an instinct to plan and prepare for what could lie ahead. For those of us who directly support just one executive, there is always this looming uncertainty about our positions when that executive exits the organization.

So, I embarked on a journey to "get ready."

First, I immediately hired someone to update my resume and LinkedIn page. Because I had been working at the same company for eight years with no intention to leave, I had not made keeping my resume and LinkedIn page updated a priority. Let this serve as your reminder to update both regularly.

Second, I am without a doubt an introvert (although many will say I don't present that way), and small talk and networking are not my favorite things to do. Because I really had not spent much time engaging on LinkedIn or doing any external networking, I set a goal to increase my LinkedIn connections to 500. Doing this not only boosted my professional network (I far exceeded that number within months), but it also gave others exposure to me, and I was asked to do my first speaking engagement. There I was, being featured on a virtual panel, "Working 9 to 5: Experiences of BIPOC Assistants," co-sponsored by BlackRock and the International Association of Administrative Professionals, dipping my toe into the administrative thought leadership world. Who could have predicted that a lockdown could lead me into the public spotlight? I certainly couldn't.

Next, I began to think about increasing engagement within my internal network. Partnering with a communications team colleague, I built the first Microsoft Teams channel dedicated to executive assistants within the division at my company. The Teams channel was a hit and fostered engagement, collaboration, and professional development among this community. Each week, I, along with other assistants, created content to share with this audience, and for the first time, there was a platform for us to connect, exchange ideas, and learn from one another.

As a result of the engagement within the Administrative Professionals Teams channel, in what seemed like a natural next step, I asked for support from my manager, the Division President, and our executive sponsor, Senior Vice President Human Resources to hold the first division-wide administrative professionals' virtual summit. It was a bit of a no-brainer, given that we were all working remotely and the costs to make this happen would be minimal. With their approval, in February 2021, we did just that. During that event, I rolled out a mission statement and purpose for the work being done with this team. I also took that opportunity to highlight how, with the onset of the pandemic, it had become critically important that we reexamine the work we do and how we show value in our "new normal." Little did I know this would spark the idea that has turned into the book you are reading now!

As I continued to find ways to intentionally expand my reach and do what I believed would prepare me for any career changes coming my way, I encountered countless individuals who, upon hearing about my experiences, would remark, "You have a story to tell." One former manager echoed this idea and reminded me of the gift I possess: my innate ability to discern the intricacies of people and situations. In that moment, her words acted as a wake-up call. It became clear that what I had deemed ordinary, others regarded as extraordinary, and it dawned on me that perhaps I did indeed have a narrative worth sharing.

I share all of that to say this: **When we learn to recognize our gifts and talents and leverage those by becoming intentional and strategic in our approach to our careers, we can often amaze ourselves with what we can accomplish.** By making a commitment to change, grow, and develop, and then making simple decisions, and taking small steps, to support that commitment, we can have a huge impact on our careers and truly transform our lives.

And so, dear reader, it is with an open heart and newfound clarity that I invite you to embark on this journey with me. In the pages that follow, we will work to uncover the untapped potential within you. Together, we will unlock the secrets to success in this new era, a time when we need to evolve and discover how our impact is poised to profoundly influence the business world.

Definition

e·volve

verb

1. develop gradually, especially from a simple to a more complex form.

Introduction

How would it feel to be heard, valued, and supported in your administrative professional position?

How would it change your life and your career to earn the income you desire and be paid for what your work is truly worth?

How would your days look different if, instead of feeling stagnant, your path ahead was one of both professional stability and growth?

In the profession of administrative support, we often find ourselves longing for more. More appreciation, more opportunities, and more recognition of our true worth. If you're reading this book, it's likely because these aspirations resonate with you. You desire to break free from the limitations that are holding you back, unlock your full potential, and create a meaningful path in your professional life.

Perhaps you're currently working in an organization where your contributions go unnoticed, or you find yourself supporting an executive who fails to recognize your capabilities. Maybe you're trapped in a cycle of stagnation, yearning for growth but feeling unseen and undervalued. It's even possible that you've reached a breaking point, contemplating a complete career shift because you've lost hope in your current circumstances.

Well, I am here to tell you, there is a way to stop feeling stuck and step into the administrative professional career that you desire. There is a path to professional, financial, and personal fulfillment, no matter how long you've been at your workplace or where you are in your career journey.

I want to let you know that it is possible to do all of this while remaining in the administrative professional field, and likely without leaving your current position.

All of this is possible. And I'm here to show you how.

Throughout this book, I'm going to bring you quite a few truths, and here's the first one: **you may have to work to earn a living, but you don't have to settle for being undervalued, underpaid, and unfulfilled.** There is a way to escape the feeling of being stunted in your career growth and embrace the career you deserve, and it's well within your reach. You hold within you the power to change your trajectory.

All it takes is for you to become an Evolved Assistant.

This book is your guide to evolution. It will lead you from the status quo to a place of intention and action and empower you to carve out your career path. Becoming an Evolved Assistant is a journey toward realizing your vision of professional growth with me as your guide. Together, we'll navigate through my **4Ms Framework**, the four principles of becoming an Evolved Assistant:

- Shift your **Mindset**. In the Mindset principle, we will focus on cultivating your attitude, outlook, mentality, and frame of mind. It is crucial to approach your personal transformation with the right mindset as it serves as the cornerstone for navigating the subsequent steps and laying the groundwork for your future success. Mindset is the space where you recognize that this journey of growth *revolves around you.*

- Master **Management**. Management is where we transition into practical application by adjusting our behavior. Here, we delve into enhancing the quality of your work by addressing your *work habits and methodologies*. This is where we refine and advance your skill set while deepening your understanding of the individuals you support and your organization's goals and objectives.

- Level up your **Marketing**. The Marketing principle, as the third component of the framework, is where you acquire the skills to *effectively promote yourself*. In Marketing, you define your personal brand and shape the narrative surrounding your role and how others perceive you.

- Prioritize **Maintenance**. In Maintenance, you integrate all the principles of the framework and put them into *sustained practice*. This is where you witness the outcomes of your efforts towards personal evolution and gain the ability to operate with confidence in your new, enhanced version of yourself, demonstrating excellence.

This framework is for all administrative professionals who want to take charge of their careers and create a better future for themselves. That list includes receptionists, coordinators, administrative assistants, executive assistants, office managers, and any of the many other titles that fall under the administrative professional umbrella. As an administrative professional myself, I know how often we can be overlooked in the professional development space and how rare it can sometimes feel that someone is speaking directly to us about our career growth. I may not have worn every hat in this profession, but I come to you from a place of firsthand experience and knowledge of the challenges you face. I share this framework with you based on what has worked for me and other administrative professionals who have overcome these challenges to build fulfilling careers.

Executives, managers, and other professionals who are supported by or benefit from the work of administrative professionals will also find Evolved Assistant useful. This book will help you better understand the administrative professional's role, develop benchmarks for your assistants, support your administrative professionals, and foster their professional development.

Finally, other decision-makers within an organization or company seeking to focus on developing their administrative teams, including Human Resource managers, will also be well-served by reading this book. To recognize the value of your administrative support staff, understand their challenges, and learn how they can overcome them will help you build a culture of empowerment among your support teams.

Now, if you're an administrative professional reading this, you might be reading all these grand promises of the benefits of evolution and think to yourself, this all sounds good, but my work environment is restrictive. It looks great, but I work for a challenging executive or on a difficult team. It would be nice, but my organization is still stuck in the 1970s. They can't imagine administrative professionals doing anything beyond making copies and retrieving coffee, and it will never change.

Listen closely. None of that matters.

Repeat after me. **None of that matters.**

Regardless of the chaos in your organization, the challenges posed by those you support, or the dysfunction among your coworkers, becoming an Evolved Assistant does not require you to alter any of it. An attempt to change your manager, colleagues, or organization's structure is beyond the scope of your job, so take that pressure off of yourself. Through Evolved Assistant, your only job is to change the one thing that you have full and complete control over, and that is you.

Becoming an Evolved Assistant is all about you. It's about showing up for yourself and taking control over your career path, your growth, and your professional development so that you can create the career you desire. Despite changes in the market, in your field, or at your organization, and whether you decide to stay in your current position or take a new one, you are the common denominator in all your professional experiences. You are in charge of your career, so it's important that you have all of the tools you need for success.

Here's another truth, and it's a harsh one: **no one is coming to save you from feeling frustrated, unheard, and undervalued in your career**. If you decide to leave your professional future in the hands of your manager or your organization, chances are high you will continue to find yourself in the same rut. The good news? It is possible to save yourself. You can steer yourself in a completely different direction on your career path, and I'm here to help.

In this book, I will provide actionable insights and practical strategies to unlock the path to improve your current career, empower you to overcome obstacles and achieve greater success and fulfillment in your professional journey.

It's a framework that I've created to combine the lessons I've learned over two decades as an administrative professional that have helped me create a fulfilling, rewarding career. I currently serve as a Regional Administrative Manager, with direct reports in multiple states, for a leading global real estate asset management firm. I stepped into this role at the time of the book's publishing, after working for more than a decade as an executive assistant for a Fortune 30 company providing direct administrative functions for two Presidents: one responsible for the largest revenue-generating division in the company and the other leading the operational arm of the organization. I held the title of Senior Manager of Administrative Services, and, in addition to providing executive support, hired, coached, trained, and managed a team of executive assistants responsible for supporting vice president level executives. I understand the executive assistant role, not just from the vantage point of my own experience, but also through the lens of helping other administrative professionals succeed in their roles, including the mindset and skills that lead to career success along with the ones that hinder it. Throughout the years, I have earned several certifications and The Admin Awards Leadership Award, taken part in programs such as the World 50 Executive Administration Program, and been a featured guest speaker in several podcasts, conferences, trainings, and other special events.

Yet, while I am proud of what I have been able to accomplish and grateful for the opportunities this career has provided, I did not write this book because the road here has been a fun-filled fairytale. I do not share my career successes to boast about accolades, but instead, to share an important lesson that has underlined every move that I've made along the way. I will get into the details of those moves within the framework, but I want to share something with you that I need you to take hold of, keep close, and allow to play in the back of your mind throughout your Evolved Assistant journey in the same way that it has in mine.

It's a lesson that I am fortunate to have learned very early, way back in the 6th grade.

A Seed is Planted

I grew up in New Orleans, Louisiana, the child of divorced parents and my mother's only child. My mother has always been and remains my biggest cheerleader. She both instilled confidence in me and demonstrated it for me throughout my childhood. She worked for the federal government for 30 years, starting as a secretary supporting the office director. I remember visiting her job as a child and watching her command the room of her colleagues with ease. It left a huge impression on me about how important it was to show up bold and confident in every space. Just watching my mother be who she was empowered me to believe that I could walk through the world in the same way.

But everyone didn't agree, and in the sixth grade, a group of girls that I had considered my closest friends were determined to let me know. One day, this group of five cornered me in the bathroom of the parochial school I attended to confront me. They huddled around me to tell me that I was too demanding, that I always wanted to be in charge, and as a result, I would no longer be a part of their friend group.

In the moment, I defended my character and argued with the group, but in the aftermath, I was hurt and began questioning myself. *Why don't they like me?* I wondered. *What have I done?* I couldn't understand what was so wrong with me that would put me in the position of being ostracized, which can be soul-crushing for a middle school girl.

When I got home that day, I told my mom about what happened. After listening to my experience, she said, "Confidence can cause discomfort for others who are not confident, but their perception of you does not mean that there is something wrong with you." She continued, "What someone else thinks of you should not dictate how you show up in the world. Their thoughts cannot stop you from being who you want to be and doing what you want to do."

I learned then that the perception others have of me does not define my value. It's a lesson I've carried with me ever since and have heard my mother's voice replaying those words in the back of my mind at many different times throughout my life and my career. In fact, it was that lesson, the confidence in my own abilities in spite of other's belief, that helped me make the very untraditional career move that landed me in the administrative profession.

A Winding Career Path

I am not what some would consider a "career administrative professional," and my road to get here was far from a direct path. After graduating from a liberal arts college in Ohio, I began a career in college recruiting at my alma mater, where I was responsible for recruiting students in Southern and Mid-Atlantic states. This required me to travel to those states, present to high school students, conduct interviews, and create on campus visitation programs for prospective students, educating them about the school and encouraging them to apply. During application season, I was responsible for reading every application in my territory and making decisions on acceptance. I had a great deal of autonomy, loved interacting with the students, and felt like I was really helping to shape the place where I had also received my education. But I was not certain back then that I could see myself in that career for a lifetime.

After spending several years in Ohio working, I wanted to get back to the South to be closer to my family, and I eventually made the move to Atlanta, where I took another job in college recruiting. Unfortunately, this new position did not ignite the passion and happiness I had in my previous one, and before long, I ended up miserable.

That misery became my motivation. It made me think harder about what I really wanted from a career and what I wanted my next move to be. I already had doubts about whether I was truly working in the career that was meant for me, and when I began to dig deeper, I realized that college recruiting wasn't it. I decided instead that I would return to a dream that I'd had since college but had never been able to figure out how to pursue.

I'll never forget the day that I went into my boss's office and slid my resignation letter across his desk. He slid it back to me and asked, "So, what are you leaving to do?"

"I'm going to beauty school."

"What?!" He exclaimed. Yes, I had decided to pursue my dream career as a cosmetologist. My employer's reaction wasn't uncommon. Many people couldn't understand why I would trade in my well-paid career to go back to beauty school, but their perceptions didn't define me. It would be far from the last time that I had to deal with others' perceptions of my career path, but thankfully, I had learned long ago not to let them get me off track.

An Unexpected Dream

The confidence that had been instilled in me at a young age gave me the courage to take the leap to bet on myself. I left my position at the college in pursuit of starting cosmetology school, but at 32 years old, I was an adult with a mortgage, bills, debt, and other financial responsibilities. I couldn't become a student without a means to support myself and needed a job schedule that would enable me to attend school in the evenings. I sat down and calculated what I needed to earn to pay the bills since I knew the chances were high that I would be earning less than I had previously. And once I figured out that number, I set out to find a position that would meet my requirements. As fate would have it, a receptionist role opened at the bank directly across the street from the cosmetology school. I applied, landed the role, and began school exactly one month after leaving my former career. Don't you love it when all of life's pieces land in place?

Shortly after starting at the bank, I was asked to apply for an assistant position supporting the vice president of retail. I took that job while going to beauty school at night. It was perfect. And it didn't take me long to realize that I really liked the work. After graduating from cosmetology school and going back into recruiting for a brief stretch when the bank was sold and our team was laid off, I found myself back in pursuit of an administrative role. While I initially still had dreams of becoming a cosmetologist, given my existing financial obligations, I knew I wouldn't be able to get a job at a salon earning minimum wage while I built my clientele.

In the meantime, I knew I enjoyed the administrative profession, so I heeded the call back to the Midwest and went to Michigan when a friend needed an assistant at a large, multi-national food corporation. I started there as a coordinator, and it was in that role that I first saw other assistants really thriving in their careers. I witnessed them doing work that I had come to love in spaces where they were moving, shaking, and making things happen. I could envision then what a future in this field looked like, and it seemed like the perfect path for me. It was there that I recognized that a career as an administrative professional was my true calling, and while I took a windy road to get here, I know that it is where I am supposed to be.

Living the Lesson

Without a doubt, I love this work. I am also great at it. Naturally drawn to structure, I'm a linear thinker, and putting processes in place comes easily to me. This really is my zone of genius, and I am immensely grateful for discovering my true passion and purpose. The opportunity to engage in fulfilling work, every day, while earning a living is even more rewarding.

But I have also experienced my share of bumps along the way. I've worked for challenging executives with whom I struggled to connect and build an effective partnership. I have worked within organizations with very little or no commitment to professional development and antiquated ideas of what people in the administrative role can contribute to an organization. And I know the feeling of being reduced to someone who can only perform task-based work without any discussion or exploration of my full capabilities.

I've shared these stories, not to just give you insight into who I am, but to also circle back around to the lesson I shared at the beginning of my journey. Each of us has taken a different path to arrive where we are in our careers, but after many years of working closely with other administrative professionals across a range of roles and organizations, I recognize that one of the biggest hurdles we face as administrative professionals is perception. Often, this perception comes in the form of colleagues, associates, and supervisors who don't understand or value our work. Sometimes, this even comes in the form of the perception we have of ourselves, our capabilities and capacity for change and whether we even view our own work as valuable.

Unfortunately, these perceptions can cause us to find ourselves trapped in careers that merely provide basic financial stability but fail to bring us fulfillment. They can result in many of us suffering from a lack of confidence and feeling voiceless in our organizations, struggling to know when to speak up and where we fit in. They cause some of us to remain fixated on our past achievements and rely solely on the skills we possessed five, ten, or even twenty years ago, with no regard for the importance of constant growth that's essential to meeting the demands of our rapidly changing future. Accepting these perceptions as fact can keep us afraid, stuck, stagnant, and unable to invest in ourselves and take the risks necessary to create the career we desire and operate with the understanding that we deserve it.

I recognize that I was fortunate in having learned not to define myself by other's perceptions as a child. Realizing that you, and only you, are in charge of defining yourself and your career journey is crucial to becoming an Evolved Assistant. Whether you grasped this lesson early on, as an adult, or are hearing it now, approaching this process with confidence and acknowledging your responsibility for your own path is essential to achieving professional fulfillment.

You may not feel like you understand this quite yet, and that's perfectly fine. The way to truly embrace these concepts is to evolve, and it's one of the things we'll work on as we work through the Evolved Assistant framework.

I have written this book because I am a champion of the work and those of us who do it. I understand that, as administrative professionals, we have a unique skill set. Some consider it a gift, and I am committed to help you cultivate the confidence to elevate your role and become recognized as a valuable contributor within your workplace. My hope is for you to realize and embrace the power of your own voice so you can achieve the personal, financial, and professional satisfaction you seek.

I acquired the lessons I share here through my journey of transitioning careers and forging a rewarding professional path in unfamiliar territory. These insights have been refined through various stages of my professional experiences.

As I navigated through my career, I often found myself yearning for a roadmap like the one presented in this book. There were times along my professional journey when I recognized the need for change or adjustment, but the path from where I stood to where I wanted to be wasn't always clear. In my early years as an assistant, I worked tirelessly for an executive who, unfortunately, never truly appreciated my contributions or invested in my personal development. She proved to be a tough nut to crack, leaving me in a constant struggle to communicate effectively with her. Her lack of engagement and ambiguity regarding her expectations made it challenging for me to gauge whether I was performing up to her standards.

Despite these hurdles, I remained committed to excellence in my work, always striving to give my best. It was disheartening to work for someone who perpetually made me feel as though I could never quite meet her standards. Looking back on those years, I find myself wishing I'd had a resource like this book, one that could have guided me in a different direction. Such a guide would have enabled me to redirect my focus away from seeking affirmation from my executive and instead prioritizing personal transformation. It would have helped me recognize that the most significant impact I could make was on my own growth and development.

As I achieved more career success, there also came a time when I felt content in my role, not really looking beyond what I was currently doing. I had a strong working relationship with my executive, my tasks were relatively straightforward, and I consistently received positive feedback for my performance. However, deep down, I developed a growing sense of boredom. I was operating on autopilot. I wasn't being challenged, and I couldn't help but feel that there was more out there for me. I knew there were more experiences to embrace, more knowledge to acquire, and more potential for higher earnings.

I began to reflect on my situation and ask myself some pivotal questions: Am I truly happy? Am I genuinely satisfied? Am I operating at my full potential? Could I be earning more? It was as if a lightbulb illuminated in my mind, igniting an intense desire for change.

I am an evolution adopter and have always been keenly aware that change is necessary for progress to take place. I also believe that embracing change requires an openness to learning and acquiring knowledge. To grow into something new, we must uncover what we don't yet know and work to bridge the gap between where we are and where we aim to be.

In my evolution journey, I've tested out the principles that became the foundation for the framework of this book. Each time I tested one, I learned something, whether it was shifting my approach to a situation mentally, becoming a better advocate for myself, developing a new skill, or enhancing a skill that I already possessed. I have also used the lessons I learned to advise others on how to apply the same principles to their work, and it has been a delight to witness their successes first-hand.

One such experience occurred when a newly promoted vice president asked me if I would be willing to mentor her executive assistant who had recently stepped into the role from the position of office receptionist. In her newly elevated role, she wanted to ensure that the type of support she was receiving was in line with that of her peers. She wanted a partner invested in her success with the skills and expertise to show up as an administrative leader and really own her work. She also wanted a bridge builder, an assistant who could represent her well as she interacted with her direct reports, peers, and manager. She needed this assistant to be open to responsibilities outside of the traditional assistant scope, like managing special projects and partnering with the communications team to create a strategic plan.

I was honored and excited for the opportunity and began what turned into a two-year mentoring relationship. During that time, the assistant was like a sponge soaking up information. She was invested and committed to learning new skills and ways to be the best at her work. Her passion was obvious, and she was eager to learn and address any mistakes to improve her performance.

The framework outlined in this book is what she and I worked through and applied, and it proved to be exactly what the assistant needed to be successful. Today, she has moved on to supporting multiple executives and is an integral part of their success on a team that is proud to boast the value of her work. She is thriving in her role and reaping the personal, professional, and financial benefits of investing in her evolution.

I feel fortunate to have played a role in helping to support her and others in reaching their professional goals through the Evolved Assistant framework, and I am equally as honored to now share it with you.

Moving Through the Framework

Keep in mind that you likely will have to take a different approach to reading the content included here than in some other books. This is not light reading material that you flip through to enjoy on a day at the beach. Transformative career evolution and re-directing your professional path is not something that happens in a few hours sitting poolside. Moreover, this content is intended to challenge you and your beliefs about what makes an extraordinary assistant. Read with the understanding that some of these topics will require self-reflection and a hard look at how you may be showing up in the workplace. It's a great idea to keep a journal as you read through the material and complete the exercises to keep track of your responses, feelings, and thoughts. You will likely discover things about yourself that will cause you to re-examine your current ways of thinking and working. It may require you to sit with yourself and reevaluate what has always been as it relates to your career. As you read and reflect, remind yourself to keep moving forward through the discomfort. Don't let it stand in the way of reaching your goal.

In the same way that I needed to learn to grow and change, I also know that the only way to realize and sustain the results you desire is to evolve. Making the necessary changes may not always be comfortable, and I have certainly had to overcome those feelings of discomfort by reminding myself that feelings are not facts. Feeling uncomfortable with something new is normal, and it doesn't mean that you are doing something wrong. It is a natural reaction to doing things you aren't used to.

Remember that evolution is not an overnight process, and neither is reading this book. Transforming your career is a big undertaking, but it doesn't have to be overwhelming. Allow the concepts that you read in the following chapters to sink in and give yourself time to practice implementing them. Instead of just reading the book end-to-end, take it section by section and practice what you've learned from one section before moving on to the next one. This book is not just based on theory; it's designed with proven, practical ways to help give you a more fulfilling career. The only way that you will be able to do that is by practicing and repeating what you've learned.

Read each chapter, take notes, work through what I like to refer to as **evolutionary exercises** and begin putting them into practice. Start small but be consistent and targeted in your approach. This is a journey, not a sprint to the finish line, and lasting change takes time and repeated behavior.

Mistakes will happen along the way. You will face roadblocks and times when you want to return to what feels comfortable. This is normal, but I encourage you to commit to continuing to move forward, even if you must take baby steps to get there. I'm here rooting for you along the way.

Finally, because this evolution is about you, only you can decide what you want your evolution to look like. The vision you have for your career is yours, and while this book will guide you toward achieving that vision, you need to get clear on what that vision is before you can start moving toward it. Take some time to map out your career path. Use the Evolutionary Exercise following this introduction to envision what becoming an Evolved Assistant looks like for you. Craft your ideal scenario for your career path and your vision for your life and remember to think big.

Be bold when it comes to your vision. Start with what you want, and don't limit it by shrinking those dreams down to what you think is possible. When you dream big and operate in excellence, you don't always know what possibilities will open up for you. My former position did not exist before I stepped into the role. My choice to continuously evolve and follow the framework that I will share with you enabled me to create opportunities for myself that I may not have known even existed. Remember, not being able to see exactly what the job title would be, especially if it doesn't exist where you are right now, is not an excuse to limit your thinking about your career or create a perceived obstacle that could prohibit your career advancement. Limiting your vision in this way will just keep you from getting to the next level and leave you trapped in a stagnant situation.

Again, this journey is about you. You've already taken the first step by picking up this book. Now take the next one by envisioning your transformation as we begin on the path through the framework.

As administrative professionals, we're used to supporting the careers of everyone around us in countless ways. But now it's time for your evolution to learn how to use all those skills to better support you. This book is a call to action, an invitation to take charge of your own destiny. It's time to step into the driver's seat of your career and navigate the path that leads to your fulfillment. The power lies within you, and I'm here to guide you every step of the way.

Are you ready to evolve? If so, I am ready to go on this journey with you. But before I get into the details of how to become an Evolved Assistant, in

Chapter One, I'll discuss why it's important to evolve and why now is the time to begin your evolution.

EVOLUTIONARY EXERCISE

Use the following prompts to map out your feelings, desired changes, and vision for yourself, your career, and your life. Take your time to think deeply and be honest with yourself.

Current Career Status

- How do you currently feel about your career as an executive assistant? Write down your thoughts, emotions, and overall satisfaction or dissatisfaction.

- What aspects of your current career do you enjoy the most? List the specific tasks, responsibilities, or experiences that bring you joy and fulfillment.

- What aspects of your current career do you find challenging or dissatisfying? Identify the areas that cause frustration, dissatisfaction, or lack of fulfillment.

Desired Changes

- What changes would you like to see in your current career? Identify specific areas or aspects you would like to improve, change, or eliminate.

- Are there any new skills or knowledge you would like to acquire to enhance your career? Consider any areas where you feel the need for growth or development.

- Are there any additional responsibilities or challenges you would like to take on? Think about opportunities for advancement or expanding your skill set.

Ideal Career Scenario

- Envision your ideal career scenario. What does it look like? Imagine a future where you are fulfilled, challenged, and satisfied with your career.

- What role or position would you ideally like to have in the future? Describe the job title, responsibilities, and any specific industry or company preferences.

- How does your ideal career align with your personal values, passions, and interests? Reflect on the factors that make your ideal career meaningful and fulfilling.

Vision for Yourself and Your Life

- How does your career fit into your overall life vision? Consider how your career aspirations align with your personal goals, values, and aspirations.

- What impact do you want to make through your career? Reflect on how you want to contribute to the world, your community, or the lives of others.

- What steps can you take to move closer to your ideal career scenario and life vision? Outline practical actions or strategies to help you progress toward your desired future.

Review your responses and look for common themes, insights, or areas where you may need to make changes or set goals. Use this exercise as a starting point to create an action plan that aligns your current career with your desired vision. Remember, your career journey is unique, and you can make changes that lead to a more fulfilling and rewarding professional life.

Why Evolve

As we embark on the journey toward becoming an Evolved Assistant, I want to share with you the story of two assistants whose paths we will follow throughout this book.

A TALE OF TWO ASSISTANTS

Meet Amanda and Tanya. By early 2020, both Amanda and Tanya have been administrative professionals for 15 years—most of their professional careers.

With so many years of experience under their belts, they both know the drill. They manage their executives' schedules and calendars, handle incoming and outgoing emails, letters, and phone calls, and serve as a point-of-contact between their executives and internal and external stakeholders. They understand the routine and go about their day doing what needs to be done to complete their work: organizing meetings and events, scheduling venues, arranging catering, preparing agendas, and distributing materials.

They also provide support for meetings and take notes. When their executives travel, they handle the arrangements by booking flights, hotels, and transportation, managing itineraries, and preparing expense reports.

Amanda, weathered by years of routine, is steadfast in her methods. She's efficient and effective in her responsibilities, relying on established workflows and processes. Comfortable in her familiar schedule, Amanda prefers the status quo. Her experience has bred a sense of contentment that dissuades her from seeking new paths or embracing unfamiliar approaches, even when faced with unexpected shifts.

Tanya, equally seasoned, is open to exploring new methods, yet lacks the confidence to venture into unfamiliar territory on her own. Leery of speaking up at the wrong time or trying something new and making a mistake, she keeps her head down and leans into those skills she's already mastered. Even in moments when she believes she might have valuable insight, she proceeds with caution and holds back, waiting for direction from her supervisor instead of speaking up or taking initiative.

While neither assistant receives much professional feedback, they rarely get complaints. They meet the expectations of those they support and perform the tasks required to fulfill their job responsibilities.

While the job is not without frustrations, Amanda and Tanya are able to keep working through the challenges. Amanda has established a routine, is comfortable in her position, and has never seriously considered a different path. While she feels her salary could be higher, it pays the bills. She is content enough with where she is and plans to remain in the administrative assistant role for the foreseeable future.

Tanya, on the other hand, has become increasingly dissatisfied with her role. Unable to pinpoint an exact cause for her discomfort, she believes that much of it results from inefficiencies within her organization. In moments of frustration, she contemplates finding a new role or even a new profession altogether, but after so many years performing the same tasks she is unsure of what she might even be qualified to do. Instead, she stays on what feels like the most comfortable path forward and accepts occasionally feeling stuck as just a part of the job.

Both assistants are worried, however, as news of the mysterious Covid-19 pandemic continues to spread. Finally, in mid-March, their companies join the majority of others in the United States and temporarily halt in-person operations.

Amanda and Tanya both take home their laptops, essential supplies, and important files. They are uncertain about how working from home will unfold since it isn't something they have done before in their current roles, but neither one of them is too worried. The company estimates they will probably only have to remain home for a couple of weeks, or maybe one month, tops.

Remember the whirlwind of uncertainty that came crashing into our lives during the early days of the Covid-19 lockdowns? It was like nothing we had ever experienced before. Not only did it wreak havoc on the personal well-being and health of millions around the world, but it also turned the professional lives of many individuals upside down. Who could have foreseen the virus' long-lasting impact, from the endless days of lockdown to the staggering economic repercussions, to the irreversible changes to how the world conducts business? All of it was a wild ride none of us saw coming.

2020 ushered in one of the biggest upheavals to our work in history, and the changes happened rapidly. Even as many companies began to return to offices either full-time or on hybrid schedules, it became clear that the nature of our work as administrative professionals would never be the same.

Prior to the pandemic, many of the core responsibilities of administrative professionals predominantly focused on task-oriented assignments that required us to be physically present alongside our managers, executives, and others we support. In addition to the organizational tasks we fulfilled, we often served as a barrier between executives and visitors or callers seeking their attention. We assisted with technological requirements. We met with them to discuss urgent matters or resolve pressing issues. And we also maintained filing systems, tracked inventory and supplies, and purchased equipment.

The pandemic caused an abrupt shift in many of our job responsibilities, yet the nature of our work has been gradually changing for decades due to an ever-evolving modern workplace, including shifts in organizational structures, increased emphasis on efficiency, globalization, constant market changes and advances in technology. But with all the versatility expected of administrative professionals in our rapidly changing environment, the perception of our role in many ways has remained similar to what it was with the rise of the "modern secretary" in the early 20th century.

A History Lesson: The Birth Of The Administrative Assistant

To give some context to this unprecedented upheaval, the current climate for administrative professionals, and the future outlook, let's take a quick look back at some of the history behind what brought us here. Knowing how some of the challenges we deal with today were created in the first place is an important step in our evolution. Understanding history helps us to understand our past, informs our present, and empowers us to shape a more promising future.

The administrative assistant role began largely due to the Industrial Revolution of the 19th century, when many businesses and organizations grew in size and complexity, causing increased demand for administrative support. The need to fill clerical positions at the onset of the Civil War followed by the advent of the typewriter, which women were considered to be better suited for at the time due to their finger dexterity, led to more women entering the field.

With women occupying 95% of secretarial roles by 1930, secretarial work became predominantly associated with women in the early 20th century. There existed a prevailing notion that women possessed the necessary skills for meticulous attention to detail, organization, and multitasking, which led to the birth of the "modern-day secretary," whose responsibilities included typing, filing, answering phones, and scheduling appointments.

Unfortunately, women were also chosen for administrative roles due to their willingness to work for low wages; this coupled with the overall devaluing of "women's work" also led to secretaries being viewed as subordinate to their male executives, often occupying lower-status positions within their organizations.

On the heels of the women's rights movement of the 1960s and 1970s, secretaries united and advocated for improved working conditions and higher compensation. This movement also brought about a shift in terminology, with the term "administrative assistant" gaining prominence to better reflect the evolving nature of the profession.

Today, being an administrative assistant entails much more than the traditional image of typing, filing, and answering phones. As dedicated administrative professionals, we play a vital role in supporting the leadership of our organizations. Despite the changing nature of our responsibilities and our titles, there still exists a persistent perception that undermines our true value. This outdated viewpoint categorizes us as subservient and belittles our work by labeling it as mundane and unimportant. In this hierarchical perspective, we find ourselves positioned low on the organizational ladder, often overlooked as leaders whose contributions directly impact the success of the company.

Among the list of the many ways we add tremendous value to our organizations, we are:

- Effective communicators: We articulate information clearly and concisely, ensuring seamless communication across various levels of the organization.

- Proactive problem solvers: Identifying areas for enhancement, we proactively create solutions to streamline processes and enhance productivity.

- Confident decision makers: Leveraging our experience and knowledge, we navigate scenarios adeptly, making decisions that significantly impact the success of our leaders and the organization.

- Relationship builders: Actively fostering connections throughout the organization, we understand the significance of networking and building relationships to facilitate smooth operations and teamwork.

Yet, instead of being valued for these skills and abilities, we are often relegated to tasks considered menial or undesirable by others. It is disheartening that many individuals within organizations remain unaware of our capabilities simply because no one bothers to inquire or recognize our full potential.

We are often left out of the conversation when it comes to professional development. While other roles perceived as adding more value to the business are coached, developed, and trained to get to the next level, within many organizations, the assistant is absent in that space. Many managers don't even think about us in terms of our own professional development. In fact, I know assistants who have gone their entire careers with no performance feedback, and I am willing to bet that you do too.

Early in my career, transitioning from recruiting to an administrative role, I faced perceptions that echoed even during interviews. Seeing my background, people often questioned my decision to pursue an administrative role, leading me to understand the lack of appreciation for administrative work. Over the years, I have encountered many situations in which I experienced the belief that some colleagues held, which was that our contributions were not as valuable as others. I have been on the receiving end of subtle implications from coworkers or executives that perhaps my education or knowledge wasn't as comprehensive as others. I have been in meetings or conversations where it was assumed that I was just someone there to take orders instead of a professional capable of offering valuable insights and expertise. It's a perception that I've strived to counter throughout my journey because I have experienced it time and again, and I know that I'm not alone.

Bridging my early experiences in an administrative role to the broader context, the challenges I encountered were not isolated incidents. Throughout my career, I observed a prevailing perception that undervalued administrative work, a sentiment reflected in various professional settings. This underlying belief, which has persisted for years, became even more apparent during the upheaval caused by Covid-19. The pandemic didn't create all the challenges that assistants have recently faced. But it did bring many of those existing issues into view. Suddenly, the problems that have persisted for decades were pulled out and placed in front of a magnifying glass, and now that we see them so clearly, there's no looking back.

The Home (Dis)advantage

Since the "modern secretary's" beginnings, an assistant's role, and much of our work, has required us to be physically in the office with our colleagues, as you know. When the Covid-19 lockdowns began, suddenly, that shared space was gone.

Many of us transitioned to remote work and our daily routines were interrupted and transformed. Providing on-site assistance to our managers, helping them with their technology, ensuring smooth operations in meeting rooms, attending to the front desk, and managing visitors became obsolete. Similarly, the need for developing travel itineraries, booking accommodations, and coordinating flights diminished due to the cancellation of in-person meetings, conferences, and other business events.

Many managers found it difficult to rely on us in a remote environment. The distance between us created a barrier, and that separation, in some instances, altered the perception of our work's value.

At the same time, many administrative professionals expressed difficulty connecting with executives and managers and struggled to understand how to support them in the virtual environment.

"When we were in the office, I kept an eye on the time and flow of meetings," expressed one assistant. "I could monitor them because I sat outside my manager's office. Often, I would physically interrupt meetings because that's what was asked of me. I knew that when meetings ran over, I needed to go in and let everyone know it was time to wrap it up. When we started working from home, that dynamic changed. I wasn't sitting right outside the meeting to check in and let them know they had five minutes or remind them of what was coming up next. They kind of just figured it out on their own."

The impact of the pandemic varied among assistants. Some of us experienced a drastic slowdown in workload, while others of us found ourselves grappling with intensified responsibilities. But several consistent themes emerged:

- An overwhelming reliance on technology, when many of our organizations had not widely embraced virtual meeting platforms. This required us to swiftly familiarize ourselves with tools to ensure effective communication between our executives and their colleagues and clients.

- The challenge of finding time and ways to communicate with our executives, who were inundated with meetings as they navigated shifting priorities, unpredictability, and uncertainty within the organizations. Instead of regular or impromptu in-person meetings with our managers, we had to rely on email, instant messaging, and phone calls.

- A compelling need to foster collaboration and support within organizations or teams. It often fell on us to find a way to replicate those dynamics in a virtual setting through online team-building activities, brainstorming sessions, and encouraging interaction among team members.

One administrative professional who led a team of 60 assistants expressed the challenges of abruptly moving from a solely in-office organization to working entirely from home. As their organization had previously incorporated very little, if any, remote work, they were not accustomed to virtual collaboration, and many employees did not have virtual meeting experience.

"During that time, a lot of us started questioning whether we were still adding value," she expressed. "I really tried to lead the team through the lens of finding unique ways to add value each day, even if it looked a little bit different than it did before. You don't have that leader that's passing by your desk, and you can't use your intuition and the nonverbal communication that's happening in person. So, in what ways can we add value and what skills do we all need to quickly learn? I'm very thankful we had a large assistant team. We began sharing skills across the team and saying, 'Hey, I learned how to do this via Zoom,' or 'I learned how to do this online with my leader.' We were sharing and being collaborative during that time and learning new skills very quickly."

Administrative professional roles obviously were not the only ones affected by this upheaval. Across the board, employees made efforts to pivot, but with the world being restricted by lockdowns, and activities moving to the virtual space, many companies lost revenue. As a result, roles within organizations were pulled under the microscope. Leaders and business owners questioned who was truly essential to their bottom line, and administrative professionals were not spared. Some executives saw the tasks they could achieve independently without their assistants and began to question, "Do I really need this individual"? As companies restructured administrative roles or reassessed staffing levels based on efficiency and cost-saving measures, assistants who hadn't cemented their value became easy to let go.

Of course, this re-evaluating and restructuring was not uniformly true. The impact varied greatly by industry, company, and region. Yet employees in roles perceived as easily replaceable were, by and large, impacted the most, and those roles have also been the slowest to recover.

In 2020, the executive assistant position was ranked number six on a list of jobs based on Glassdoor data that suffered the biggest decrease in job openings as a result of Covid-19. Executive assistant job openings declined by 55 percent between October 2019 and October 2020. Andrew Chamberlain, Ph.D., and former Chief Economist at Glassdoor, said, "As the global pandemic shifts consumer behavior and workplace habits, certain jobs like audiologists, executive assistants, and coaches may not return en masse for years, if ever."

Now don't panic. These statistics aren't here to spell out doom and gloom for an administrative professional's career path. They aren't included to make you pack up your desk and head for the hills. The encouraging news is that although the pandemic posed various challenges to our perceived value, it also presented us with fresh and unique opportunities to demonstrate our worth, provided we were prepared to embrace the change and transform along with the challenges.

In my own experience, as the pandemic progressed, I continued to connect with assistants to understand on multiple levels the challenges we faced, the opportunities that were present, and the skills that spelled the difference between success and failure in an assistant's career.

Gone were the days when assistants could rely on performing the same task-based duties they had been assigned for 15 or 20 years and still be regarded as valuable to the organization. Administrative professionals were now realizing that those tasks no longer held the same level of significance or contributed as substantially to the company's growth or profitability as had once been the case.

For example, many call center operations sent employees to work from home during the pandemic, and several chose to permanently transition those call centers to a fully remote workforce. The staff, managers, and directors who had worked in brick-and-mortar locations were no longer able to rely on the support of administrative assistants for managing employee engagement activities, organizing on-site events, handling vendor relations, ordering office supplies, coordinating food orders, overseeing facilities, and arranging gifts and giveaways. With the transition to remote work, the need for someone to take care of these tasks within the physical building diminished, and as companies worked to reduce costs, widespread staff reductions took place, with some organizations letting go of up to half of their administrative staff.

But assistants who were able to adapt to new circumstances and be proactive in providing value were the ones who found opportunity. Those who thrived during this time:

- Discovered new avenues to support their teams and executives.

- Leveraged technology to maintain effective communication and collaboration.

- Recognized the importance of their role in driving organizational success.

- Were intentional about engaging their teams, managers, and executives virtually.

- Mastered the art of building strong professional relationships and ensuring productive interactions.

- Committed to continuous growth and learning.

The era of adhering to the same practices we've followed for decades has come to an end, and merely hoping to be recognized for the tasks we perform is no longer sufficient. To demonstrate your worth as an administrative professional in today's competitive job market, adaptation is crucial, which means being able to adopt a fresh perspective on the work you undertake and to adjust how you present yourself. Embracing the lessons learned during this unique and transformative period, which one could refer to as a liminal experience, became paramount for forging a successful path forward.

Liminality is defined as "the state of being in-between or something that is in a state of transition." Traditionally, it was used as an anthropology term, most often in conjunction with cultural rites of passage, to define a transitional period between one phase and the next. For instance, young members of a tribe being put through tests and trials as their entry into adulthood would be categorized as having a liminal experience.

A Harvard Business Review article categorized the Covid-19 Pandemic as a liminal experience—an in-between period, after which we had to navigate a world that was different than the one that existed before[1].

During the height of the pandemic, tasks which were once routinely performed by administrative professionals were no longer feasible, but this shift presented opportunities to explore an entirely different set of skills. We needed to be ready to respond to different challenges day-by-day, and sometimes moment-by-moment, as the parameters of the pandemic were constantly changing. One crucial skill many of us needed to develop was a strong grasp of virtual meeting technologies.

In the virtual office setting, it also became essential for us to expand our scope to include a more strategic approach to our work, and those of us who proactively embraced a tech-focused mindset found ourselves at an advantage. We gained visibility, recognition, and appreciation, and as a result, many executives now require administrative professionals to step up as leaders and strategic partners in work management rather than simply waiting for instructions.

"What triggered me to try to evolve even more was at first we thought we would be back in the office within a couple of weeks," voiced one assistant. "Weeks turned into more weeks, and then months, and I thought, I need to solidify my existence here in the company. I need to become something that can add value so that it justifies the pay for my job."

The pandemic brought the critical importance of evolution to the forefront and put the need for change in the spotlight, but the importance persists even now that its impact is in our rearview mirror.

The Generational Nature of Leadership

Take a moment to observe your company's landscape. The face of organizational leadership is always undergoing a shift towards a younger generation. We've seen how, as older employees approach retirement age, the next generation starts taking on leadership positions, and soon another generation will be rising up the ranks. This never-ending cycle of change in the age of leadership brings along different expectations for everyone, including administrative professionals, and requires us to adapt accordingly. This is especially evident with technological advances and younger generations helping leaders adapt to those changes. New expectations also arise when administrative activities valued by older generations no longer hold the same significance for younger leaders.

Recently, I had a conversation with an executive assistant who found herself facing a unique challenge when the executive she supported for many years, a person in their 60s, retired. The assistant's new leader, in her late 30s, came in with a completely different working style compared to the previous executive. The new executive, who is proficient in many of the tasks the assistant had previously performed for the former executive, values an assistant who can serve as a sounding board, actively participate in meetings, offer feedback, and demonstrate a deep understanding of the business. The assistant also needs to be willing to take initiative, independently accomplish tasks, and feel empowered and confident enough to handle situations autonomously. To show up in this new way, after years of working under different expectations, overwhelmed the executive assistant, and led her to question her ability to thrive in this new environment. Yet, had she understood the importance of evolution and the need to show up as a strategic partner and adopt a new set of responsibilities, she could actually have seen this as an exciting opportunity for career growth.

The nature of leadership is always changing. A decade from now, another generation will step into leadership roles, and technology will further advance and affect our day-to-day work. This ever-changing technological landscape adds another layer to our profession. It requires a willingness to learn new technology and sharpen our skills, and the flexibility to adapt to new approaches quickly, understanding that what we learned yesterday may be obsolete tomorrow, and doing our best work means being able to embrace change.

The one thing you can always count on is that things will change. By learning the importance of adapting and seeing the opportunities that those changes present, you will continue to open new doors for yourself and enjoy a more fulfilling career.

In the coming chapters, we will walk through the process of becoming an Evolved Assistant, but first, let's explore what an Evolved Assistant is (and what it isn't).

What Is An Evolved Assistant

A TALE OF TWO ASSISTANTS

Amanda and Tanya sat in their respective home offices, staring at their computer screens, feeling a mix of anxiety and confusion. The pandemic had forced their company to transition to a remote working environment, and they were struggling to adapt. Both were concerned about their relevance in this new world where face-to-face interactions and the tasks that were once a big part of their day-to-day were no longer happening.

Amanda, who had always excelled at building personal connections, found herself at a loss. She had built her career on her ability to read people, understand their needs, and provide personalized solutions. But now, with most interactions happening through video calls and emails, she felt disconnected and uncertain about how to make an impact.

Tanya, on the other hand, was known for her exceptional organizational skills and attention to detail. Even with her feelings of stagnation with her organization, she thrived in the fast-paced office environment, managing projects, and coordinating team efforts. But now, with everyone working from their homes, the structure and rhythm she was accustomed to seemed to have vanished. She wondered how she could still contribute effectively without the usual cues and collaborative atmosphere.

As days turned into weeks and weeks turned into months, Amanda and Tanya became increasingly frustrated in their attempts to navigate the remote working environment. Amanda's once vibrant personality and ability to connect with clients were stifled by the virtual barrier, leaving her feeling detached and ineffective. Despite her best efforts, she struggled to recreate the personal touch that had defined her success. Tanya, too, faced mounting frustrations as her organizational prowess seemed to lose its impact in the absence of face-to-face collaboration. The lack of structure and the constant need to adapt to the ever-changing circumstances left her longing for the familiar rhythms of the office. Both assistants yearned for a return to their normal dynamic environment and wondered how they could find their footing in this new world, that seemed to diminish their strengths.

The onset of Covid-19 caused our two assistants to struggle to find their place in the new virtual world. To move beyond feeling frustrated and stuck, they would have to evolve.

But what does it mean to evolve?

As noted in the preface, evolution is defined as the gradual development of something, especially from a simple to a more complex form. The concept of evolution transcends various domains. Biological evolution refers to different organisms and how environmental conditions can alter a species' biological makeup over time. Cultural evolution encompasses aspects like traditions, languages, practices, and beliefs and how developments in these areas can cause change on a societal level. Technological evolution is rapid in our present era and involves innovation around existing systems, leading to more advanced technological inventions and use.

Becoming an Evolved Assistant is a form of personal evolution, and much like the previous examples, it involves going from wherever you are right now to a more advanced form. It entails shedding the modes of operation that have kept you stuck in your career and taking on a new approach to succeed in the future.

Much like in biological evolution, the catalyst to evolve often originates from some external circumstance that forces evolution to become necessary. For instance, before the Industrial Revolution, most peppered moths in England had light-colored wings, which allowed them to be camouflaged against the trees where they rested, protecting them from predators. As industrialization progressed, pollution from factories darkened the tree trunks with soot, making the light-colored moths more visible.

In this altered environment, a genetic variation occurred, resulting in moths with darker wings that were better camouflaged against the newly darkened tree trunks. These moths were more likely to survive and reproduce, passing on their dark-winged trait to their offspring. Over time, the number of dark-winged moths increased significantly, while the light-winged moths became less common.

This shift in the moth population's appearance is a classic example of evolution driven by an external event. What kept the moths safe and successful in the past was no longer going to provide the same result in the future, so their survival depended on them being able to change.

Why this science lesson? Because just like the moth, external events have and will continue to change the conditions in which we operate and alter the skills we need to succeed. You can no longer operate as you did in the past and think that you will get successful results in the future.

What got you here won't get you there.

If you want to excel in your career, this principle is vitally important to remember, no matter where your path takes you. Even if you feel like you've had a successful career as an administrative professional and everything you've done up to this point has worked, those past achievements are not a clear indicator of future success.

This may sound like a problem, but it is an exciting opportunity for professional growth.

I had a conversation with an assistant who was juggling the support of 12 to 15 executives prior to the pandemic, handling tasks like travel arrangements, expense reports, and meeting coordination.

"But when the pandemic hit, a lot of that changed right away," he shared. "There was no travel, no expenses, and no in-person meetings. Prior to the pandemic, I was kind of spread thin over several leaders, and a lot of that went away. I had to evolve and become more engaged in staff and project meetings, understanding our department's functions and how I could contribute to the team's goals. I used to be hands on, tied to my desk, always available. But the executives have become more self-sufficient, and don't need me to be constantly physically present. In the last couple of years, I've grown accustomed to communicating as needed. This has allowed me to transition into a role player and team contributor and to participate more in meetings. Now, it's not a big deal if I'm not sitting at my desk when they need me; we communicate via Teams, and we're free to work from our desks or offices."

His decision to adapt to the changing environment brings me to an important aspect of the evolution process. Now, in many ways, your evolution as an assistant is similar to the other types of evolution I detailed above, with one important difference: choice. External change is inevitable. Just like the moths had no say over whether their trees would go from light to dark, the pandemic was going to progress, with or without your approval. But unlike those moths sitting on a tree with their futures determined entirely by whether they possessed certain genes, your ability to change is a choice.

Here is another concept to keep at the front of your mind: **Change is inevitable, but personal growth is a choice.**

Change, whether it is global or on an organizational level, is often something you have little to no control over. You can't control whether there will be another pandemic, whether your company continues remote work or not, whether your company's leadership gets shaken up, advancing technologies, or even whether that coworker that you don't like working with chooses to leave or stay.

You can, however, decide what you do when those changes present themselves. You can take those changes in the outside world, whether negative or positive, and choose to grow. You can make the conscious choice to view these changes as an opportunity to evolve and provide a platform for your future success.

Earlier, I defined evolution as the gradual development of something, especially from a simple to a more complex form. An Evolved Assistant gradually develops the mindset and skills necessary to adapt to their environment to become a more advanced version of themselves.

Many administrative professionals experience common frustrations.

- Feeling stuck in your role
- Not being given the higher-level responsibilities that you know you are capable of
- Being overlooked and not given respect for your contributions
- Receiving little to no professional development
- Feeling like it's extremely difficult to earn more or get promotions
- Rarely receiving performance feedback

Do any of these apply to you? What feelings do these challenges evoke?

Many administrative professionals can experience a range of emotions in their workplace.

- A lack of perceived value in their organization
- Disrespected
- Unheard
- Under-appreciated
- Disempowered
- Stunted in their professional growth

And while having moments of job dissatisfaction is normal, even for those who enjoy their jobs and careers, constantly feeling this way is a sign that something needs to change. If you feel this way frequently in your position, it's time to work on changing you.

Before we proceed, I want to make sure you understand and truly believe that transformation is possible. Tell yourself and reinforce this truth in your mind. Personally, I have developed the habit of retraining my inner voice. If I want to make a change in my life, instead of focusing on the negative self-talk or the reasons that would prevent me from accomplishing that change, I acknowledge the thought and tell myself the exact opposite.

Accept and believe that you can grow your career, be seen as a real contributor to those you support and add value to your organization. Even if, at some point, you embark on another career path, achieving this mindset will always be critical to your future success.

Being an Evolved Assistant requires you to be mindful and intentional about your personal and professional growth and development. When you make the goal your own evolution and commit to providing value regardless of what is going on in your organization or in the world, you will advance in your career. As Georgetown University professor Cal Newport says in his book "So Good They Can't Ignore You," you need to, "Put aside the question of whether your job is your true passion, and instead turn your focus toward becoming so good they can't ignore you."[2]

The Attributes of an Evolved Assistant

What does being an Evolved Assistant look like in practice? Well first, let me provide some examples of what an Evolved Assistant is NOT.

- Views themselves only as someone who receives and performs orders and directives

- Waits on someone "higher up" to tell them what to do

- Is not forward thinking

- Cannot connect the dots

- Does not "live" in the details

- Does not have systems in place

- Does not see themselves in a role that contributes to the bottom line

- Is not clear on how the work they do saves time and increases productivity for those they support

- Is not interested in change or learning anything new

- Is not innovative in finding new and more ways to add value

- Is not paying attention to the business, how it's evolving, and how they can contribute to that evolution

- Is emotionally charged and allows their feelings to dictate their behavior

Do you know anyone like this? Do you see yourself in any of these attributes? It's okay if you do, because transforming from this state into a better one is the reason why you're here. By following the framework outlined in this book, you will be able to embody the attributes of an Evolved Assistant.

It's important to recognize that becoming an Evolved Assistant doesn't mean perfecting every one of these aspects 100 percent of the time, but instead is a commitment to striving toward continuous improvement in these areas.

An Evolved Assistant

- Is passionate about the work

- Understands how to receive directives, ask clarifying questions, and proceed with execution excellence

- Is confident (not perfect) enough to make decisions

- Balances living in the details with being aware of the big picture, vision, goal, and end result

- Thinks ahead to prepare for the future

- Anticipates needs

- Knows what they do well and shows up to flex that muscle where appropriate

- Is always learning, reading about their industry, and understanding their organization's products and services

- Seeks constructive feedback

- Identifies where they contribute to the bottom line

- Is confident enough to ask for help when they need it

- Is a master of systems

- Is innovative

- Knows the value of partnering with other assistants to advance their skills and knowledge base

- Understands the importance of technological skills and is comfortable learning new tools

- Is a time saver and strategic partner for those they support

- Can manage their emotions and not take things personally

By the end of this book, you will be well-positioned to take control of your future and build your desired career using the four transformational principles as you embark on your career as an Evolved Assistant.

By simply picking up this book and making a point of reading it, you have already taken the very first step to becoming an Evolved Assistant, and that is knowing when you need to seek additional support to grow. The belief that growth is possible and purposely pursuing the tools to aid in that growth is a marker of someone who is already looking to evolve. It takes guts to acknowledge that your current way of operating can only take you so far. It also takes courage to seek out and implement the knowledge that will help propel you forward.

So, with that in mind, let me congratulate you! You are already making strides by gaining the knowledge and support you need for your journey.

I'm proud of you. You're now ready to begin your Evolved Assistant journey in the next chapter with the Mindset principle.

As you explore the principles to come, remember the two keys discussed earlier in this chapter, and hold them in the back of your mind:

- What got you here won't get you there.// add-subtract

- Change is inevitable, but growth is a choice.

EVOLUTIONARY EXERCISE

Take a look at the attributes listed under the category of what an Evolved Assistant is not. Do you possess any of those traits? Now look at the attributes listed under the Evolved Assistant category. Are there features of an Evolved Assistant that you already feel you do well? Pull out your journal and write down your thoughts.

Think about the following questions as they pertain to your career.

- What qualities do you believe contribute to a great attitude and a strong work ethic?

- How do you navigate and adapt during times of change?

- In what ways do you apply critical thinking skills to support your team or executive effectively?

- Could you describe your involvement in decision-making processes and your contributions to the conversation?

- What are some examples of decisions you've made that positively influenced your executive's or team's productivity?

CHAPTER SUMMARY

- While we can't control external changes, we can decide how to respond and grow from them.

- Common frustrations among administrative professionals include feeling stuck, undervalued, and lacking opportunities for growth. These feelings signal a need for personal evolution.

- An Evolved Assistant possesses attributes such as confidence, anticipation of needs, continuous learning, emotional management, and the ability to contribute strategically to their organization.

- The journey to becoming an Evolved Assistant involves four key principles: Mindset, Management, Marketing, and Maintenance.

- Recognizing the need for growth and seeking knowledge to aid that growth is the first step in evolving as an administrative professional.

- Two key concepts to remember:
  - What got you here won't get you there.
  - Change is inevitable, but growth is a choice.

- Self-reflection on current attributes and areas for improvement is crucial in beginning the evolution process.

Mindset

A TALE OF TWO ASSISTANTS

Now months into their new work-from-home world, Amanda and Tanya continued to feel overwhelmed by the sudden shift in their work environment. With no clear timeline for their offices reopening, it began to feel less and less likely that there would be a return to "normal" any time soon. They had begun to appreciate some things about the new remote environment, like no longer having to commute to work in the morning, but they continued to struggle in other areas. Not only did the lack of personal interaction with their colleagues and executives sometimes feel isolating, but every day also seemed to beg the questions: how do I remain relevant, and where do I fit in?

After realizing the need for support and guidance, Tanya decided to seek help. She actively connected with other administrative professionals to see how they were managing the new virtual world and searched for resources that could assist her in adapting to the remote work setup more effectively. During her search, she began listening to podcasts, which promised to provide valuable insights and strategies for thriving in the evolving work landscape. Intrigued, she began diving into more professional development materials, hoping to gain knowledge and direction.

Meanwhile, Amanda held a different perspective. After all, this change was temporary. At some point, things would return to normal. In the meantime, she knew that with her experience and abilities, she could navigate the challenges of remote work on her own until everyone returned to the office. She considered herself an "expert" administrative assistant and felt that her accumulated knowledge and skills were sufficient to tackle any obstacles she might encounter. She would buckle down, keep doing what she had been doing, and ride out the challenges until things changed.

Amanda and Tanya's companies began implementing new systems to help streamline their organizations' activities. Among these was a new project management software to keep track of the many tasks now taking place virtually. In theory, this program would make their work flow more smoothly, but everyone would soon discover that mastering the new technology also came with a steep learning curve.

Tanya approached the situation with an open mind and a positive attitude. She recognized that the new software could offer opportunities for her to excel and make a valuable contribution to her team. Tanya took the initiative to learn the ins and outs of the software, attending training sessions and seeking additional resources to deepen her understanding.

As Tanya became more proficient in the project management software, she discovered ways to optimize workflows and improve team efficiency. She actively shared her knowledge with her manager and colleagues, offering guidance on utilizing the software's features to their advantage. Tanya's proactive approach and willingness to embrace change resulted in increased productivity and smoother project execution for the entire team.

On the other hand, Amanda was immediately frustrated by the introduction of the new software. Not only did she feel that the technology was unnecessarily complex, but it also duplicated some of her tasks, like checking in with the team about project status updates and compiling reports for her manager. Instead of seeing the introduction of the project management software as an opportunity, she began to question the necessity of the software and how it might negatively impact her role. Self-doubt and insecurity set in, causing Amanda to retreat and withdraw from actively engaging with the new tool.

Amanda's mindset about the software and her reluctance to adapt led to her falling behind in utilizing it effectively. She struggled to grasp its functionalities and failed to keep up with the evolving work processes. Soon, Amanda's manager and colleagues grew frustrated with her inability to contribute to the team's efforts and adapt to the new way of working.

In this chapter, we're tackling your mindset, also known as your own thoughts. We'll confront those little voices in your head that sometimes try to dim your shine. Here is where you acknowledge that, while you may not always be able to alter your work environment, you possess the power to shift how you present yourself through your thoughts and actions. Through the Mindset principle, I challenge you to rewrite the script and create an entirely new narrative for your journey. But beware: your mindset is often the toughest to address and change.

Mindset encompasses your attitude, perspective, mentality, and the fundamental beliefs that shape your being. This is where you learn to redirect the mirror from your organization back to yourself, taking charge of your career, growth, and personal evolution.

It serves as the underlying structure that guides your actions, whether consciously or unconsciously. To change our mindset can be a challenging process since our mindset is often shaped by unconscious influences that we carry with us throughout our entire professional journey, without even realizing it. In fact, much of our mindset about work and our careers was likely created well before we even started working. Things like confidence, belief in our ability to learn and grow, and our perception of ourselves and others go all the way back to our childhood. Once we become adults and have been operating with a particular mindset, it's only natural that altering our entire mentality becomes a real challenge.

The road to do this can feel difficult, but it is necessary, and it is most certainly possible. Psychologist Dr. Carol Dweck, whose findings in the mindset arena we will explore later in this chapter, emphasizes this point, stating, "Most experts and great leaders agree that leaders are made, not born, and that they are made through their own drive for learning and self-improvement."[3] By changing your mindset, you begin to implement the daily practice of welcoming bounty into your life and believing that you are worthy of professional success. With this mental shift, you know that at any point, you can change how you think about your career and put in motion the things required to create your desired results. It is understanding that although you may not see all of the answers, possess all of the skills, and have all of the experience to step into the career you want at this moment, as an Evolved Assistant, you know that acquiring what you need to get to the next level is a gradual process, and with the right, targeted approach, you will definitely get there.

I used to view myself, and others in similar roles, as individuals solely responsible for handling tasks in the background. We went about our duties, ensuring our executives had everything they needed and generally staying within the confines of our basic responsibilities. While these tasks were unquestionably essential, I began to realize that this narrow focus was a reduction of my own skills and abilities, limiting my own potential and the broader impact I could have.

I began to experiment with how I showed up.

- Offering suggestions to improve processes
- Calling out more efficient ways to execute tasks
- Identifying opportunities to free up time for my executive

And in the course of changing my approach to how I did my job, I gradually shifted my mindset. These experiences prompted me to think beyond the confines of my traditional role and encouraged me to envision a broader scope of responsibilities. I came to recognize that even in a support function, we possess opportunities to exhibit leadership and contribute significantly to our organizations. This shift in perspective has been incredibly rewarding as I've progressed throughout my career.

In one instance, I supported an executive who relied on me to create PowerPoint presentations. He would draw lines, graphs, and stick figures on paper (yes, it was really that rudimentary) to convey complex ideas to include in the presentations through these sketches and drawings. Although initially challenging to decipher, I used my expertise to decode these visuals, translating them into compelling presentations suitable for the intended audience.

Years earlier, I had taken a course in Slideology by Nancy Duarte, that focused on transforming data-heavy content into visually engaging presentations.[4] This training became instrumental as I applied graphic approaches to craft slides that resonated with the company's decision-makers. I remember one such decision-maker coming up to me shocked after my executive presented using a PowerPoint that I created in a meeting. "Did you create that?" they asked, knowing that creating presentations was not my executive's strong suit, but somehow in awe that I possessed the skill to do it myself. Back to those old perceptions again.

Yet I knew that my knowledge, ability, and the mindset I cultivated to grow beyond perceptions and pre-defined notions of my work contributed to the successful delivery of these presentations and ultimately facilitated informed decision-making. Elevating this one task highlighted the impact an administrative professional can have beyond the conventional realm of the role.

The Mindset principle holds the potential to truly reshape your perspective. I want to prepare you for a professional journey, one that might gently shake the foundation of your thoughts in a liberating way. This isn't just about learning how to get the next promotion or raise; it's about nurturing a mindset about your career that resonates deeply and aligns with your aspirations.

Growth vs. Fixed

Developing a growth mindset is the key essential building block to knowing that evolution is achievable.

You may have heard of the term "growth mindset," which has been a popular concept in corporate cultures for some time. But it originated with the work of Dr. Carol Dweck. Her studies demonstrated that individuals with a growth mindset, those who believe their abilities can be developed, consistently outperformed those with a fixed mindset. Dweck's research showed that a growth mindset leads to increased motivation, effort, and resilience, ultimately leading to higher achievement levels.

How do you determine the difference between the two? In short, a fixed mindset believes that our intelligence and abilities are innate and static, while a growth mindset believes that intelligence and abilities can be developed and improved through learning and effort.

Characteristics of a Fixed Mindset

- Avoiding challenges: Those with a fixed mindset tend to avoid challenges because they fear failure or believe that their abilities are fixed and cannot be improved. They may prefer to stick to tasks and activities they are already comfortable with, avoiding new and unfamiliar experiences.

- Perceiving new things as too hard: People with a fixed mindset often perceive new tasks or skills as too difficult and believe they lack the necessary innate talent or intelligence to succeed. This perception can discourage them from trying new things or taking on challenging endeavors.

- Expecting rewards without effort: These individuals may have a sense of entitlement, expecting rewards, recognition, or success without putting in the necessary effort. They may believe their abilities alone should guarantee positive outcomes rather than recognizing the importance of hard work and perseverance.

- Ignoring feedback: Fixed mindset individuals tend to ignore or dismiss feedback, particularly if it implies that they need to improve or change. They may see feedback as a personal attack or criticism rather than an opportunity for growth. Consequently, they miss out on valuable insights that could help them develop their skills and abilities.

- Feeling threatened by others' success: People with a fixed mindset may feel threatened or envious when they witness the success of others. Instead of viewing others' achievements as inspiration or evidence of what is possible, they may see them as a reflection of their own inadequacy. This mindset can lead to a competitive or resentful attitude toward others' accomplishments.

Characteristics of a Growth Mindset

- Embracing challenges: Pursuing challenges and viewing them as opportunities for growth and learning are indicators of a growth mindset. Those with a growth mindset understand that facing challenges can lead to personal development as they push themselves beyond their comfort zones and acquire new skills and knowledge.

- Believing in the capacity to learn: People with a growth mindset firmly believe in their ability to learn and improve, even if they don't possess certain knowledge or skills at present. They have confidence in acquiring new information, developing new competencies, and expanding their understanding through effort, practice, and continuous learning.

- Recognizing effort as the path to mastery: Understanding that mastery and expertise come through dedicated effort and perseverance is key to developing a growth mindset. Individuals with a growth mindset acknowledge that progress and improvement require sustained practice, hard work, and a willingness to embrace challenges. They are committed to putting in the necessary time and effort to achieve their goals.

- Embracing feedback as a learning opportunity: Those with growth mindset value feedback as a valuable source of information and guidance. They are open to receiving feedback from others as they recognize that it can provide insights into areas for improvement and help them develop their skills. They are receptive to feedback, even if it involves constructive criticism, and use it to enhance their growth and performance.

- Finding inspiration in others' success: People with a growth mindset find inspiration and motivation in the achievements and successes of others. They see others' accomplishments as evidence of what is possible and view them as role models to learn from. They are not threatened by others' success but rather celebrate it and use it as a source of inspiration to strive for their own goals.

If you read these characteristics and find that you possess some or all the qualities listed under a fixed mindset, don't worry. One essential to change and elevate your mindset is recognizing that a fixed mindset can be transformed into a growth mindset by implementing the right tools and strategies. You can develop the characteristics that help foster a mindset of continuous growth, resilience, and personal development. As Dweck says in her book, "The New Psychology of Success," "Mindsets are just beliefs. They're powerful beliefs, but they're just something in your mind, and you can change your mind."[5]

Here's an example that I imagine some of you can relate to. Over the years, I've worked in organizations that frequently switched communication and data tracking technologies, such as moving from teleconferencing to video conferencing and making changes in expense reporting tools. I have been fortunate that these organizations took the initiative to provide training sessions for administrative staff who would be using these technologies on behalf of our executives. During and after these sessions, it was evident who approached the information with a fixed mindset versus a growth mindset.

Individuals with a fixed mindset often expressed resistance, saying things like, "Why do we have to switch when the old technology or tool is working fine?" or "This new process seems too complicated; I'm not sure I can handle it without assistance," or even, "I'd rather stick with the old technology, can I continue using it?"

In contrast, those with a growth mindset reacted differently, embracing the opportunity to learn something new. They might say, "Wow, it's great to have the opportunity to learn something new. This may be a challenge, but once I learn it, I will have gained a new skill that will help me be more effective in supporting my executive."

You see the difference there?

A growth vs. a fixed mindset is not always an all-or-nothing endeavor. People may be more comfortable with a growth mindset in some areas like connecting with colleagues or learning new processes but have a fixed mindset in others like understanding new technology. Some may be adaptable to levels of change but revert to a fixed mindset when the pace of change picks up and feels overwhelming. Exhibiting characteristics of a fixed or growth mindset in one area doesn't necessarily translate to every other, and chances are, in some area, there's room for your mindset to grow.

The journey towards this mindset growth is seldom a linear progression. You'll begin to see and realize that much of what you're learning to master isn't guiding you on a straight line toward evolution. Instead, you begin a cycle of continuous improvement. As you embrace a growth mindset, you will become more confident in your ability to grow. That confidence will empower you to partner with your colleagues and make decisions, further validating the power of a growth mindset and leading you back through that cycle, growing stronger each time.

The following exercise will help you assess your current mindset and lay the foundation to either begin operating with a growth mindset or to enhance your mindset, wherever it might be. Remember, this exercise is for you. No one else is seeing your reflections. You aren't being graded on it, so be completely open and honest with yourself and your feelings about each situation. Try not to judge your answers or change your response to reflect what you think you should have done. It's okay if where you are right now doesn't fully align with a growth mindset. You need to be clear about where you are before you can start mapping out where you want to be.

Evolutionary Exercise

Write down three recent situations or challenges you have encountered at work.

For each situation, ask yourself the following questions.

- Did I approach this situation with the belief that my abilities were fixed and unchangeable? In what ways?

- Did I view this situation as an opportunity for growth and improvement? In what ways?

- How did I respond to feedback or criticism related to this situation?

- Did I feel threatened or envious when witnessing the success of others in this context?

- In what ways did I embrace the challenge and see it as an opportunity for learning?

Reflect on your answers and note any patterns or tendencies that emerge. Consider whether your responses align more with a fixed or growth mindset.

Characteristic Analysis

Now, review the characteristics of both fixed and growth mindsets outlined in the chapter. For each characteristic, identify which resonates more strongly with your own thoughts, behaviors, and beliefs.

Mindset Identification

After completing the reflection and characteristic analysis, take a step back and evaluate your overall mindset tendencies. Do you notice a leaning towards a fixed or growth mindset based on your responses and analysis?

Intention for Growth

Regardless of your initial identification, remember that mindsets can be transformed and change over time. Commit to cultivate a growth mindset by setting an intention to embrace challenges, seek continuous learning, recognize the importance of effort and perseverance, and find inspiration in the success of others.

Confidence

I introduced the concept of confidence early in this book through my personal story because confidence is fundamental to our growth. As we've discussed, confidence enables us to perform at our best, even when others' opinions may cause self-doubt. It facilitates clear and effective communication in our roles, allowing us to assertively express our ideas. Confidence empowers us to make decisions and gives us the determination to overcome mistakes and challenges. With confidence, we recognize ourselves as leaders in our space and understand ourselves to be essential contributors to our organizations. Furthermore, a confident demeanor conveys competence and capability, and can instill trust and credibility.

Like me, some were able to hone their confidence growing up, and some folks are just naturally confident, but for others, confidence needs a bit of polishing and nurturing. There is nothing wrong with needing a confidence boost. Most of us do from time to time, and this section is designed to give you the tools needed to develop your confidence in order to grow.

In my experience collaborating with administrative professionals in various roles, I have observed a common challenge related to confidence. Much of this comes from our concept of hierarchy. Many assistants believe that job titles are an inherent indicator of expertise. We accept the notion that those we support know more than we do, which can create a lack of confidence in our own skills and abilities.

One important message I convey to my team, which I want to share with you now, is that the belief that executives automatically know more than you do simply because of where their position ranks in an organization is nonsense! As administrative professionals, we are subject matter experts in our work. Your company's executives may possess more business knowledge, and others in your department may be well-versed in their respective business functional areas, but as an administrative professional, you are an expert in the service you provide—an area of expertise that others, including the executives you support, may find challenging.

One of my areas of expertise is the ability to manage time effectively, even in the most chaotic circumstances. I remember when an executive I supported had one of the most daunting days ahead of her. She had back-to-back meetings and a speaking engagement, and she needed to find time to review a presentation for an upcoming meeting with her manager. There was no way she would be able to get all of this done and have a moment to eat or even take a bio break. So, I sprang into action - printed her schedule, sat down with her to understand what her priorities were for the day, and did what I knew how to do best. I identified meetings that could be shortened, ones in which she could have a proxy attend on her behalf and postponed any of the non-essential tasks.

With a plan, I was able to orchestrate a well-structured day for her. I also kept an eye on the clock to ensure she remained on time, built in some breaks, and grabbed her lunch so she could have a moment to process and stay energized throughout the day.

I am sure you, too, can point to the areas in which you shine. By identifying and honing these skills, you build confidence. Perhaps you are not well-versed in financial analysis or creating balance sheets, but you excel at implementing processes to improve time efficiency and enhance productivity. Focusing on what you know and continually improving those skills fosters confidence.

If you need some help identifying these areas of expertise, plenty of tools can assist you in determining where your skills and abilities lie.

- Self-assessment tools, like Myers-Briggs Type Indicator (MBTI), CliftonStrengths, and DISC Assessment are all tools to help identify strengths, personality traits, and behavioral styles to gain more insights into areas where you excel.

- Skills assessments on websites like Indeed, Coursera, edX, Khan Academy, Brainbench and ProProfs offer a variety of tests to assess your skills in different areas.

- You can use your professional network, whether in-person or through networks like LinkedIn, to gain feedback from others about your professional strengths.

- Past performance may identify areas where you consistently received praise and recognition.

- To gain even deeper insights into your professional strengths and action plans for how to leverage them, a career coach or mentor can provide personalized guidance.

Being well-informed of the needs of those you support is its own type of skill which also helps build confidence and empowers you to make decisions. For example, as an Executive Assistant, I understood my former executive's work enough to make decisions regarding calendar management and screening requests. I knew enough about his business to determine whether his time was best spent on a particular matter or should be redirected elsewhere. Given the constant stream of individuals demanding his time and input, my grasp of his business allowed me to assess if someone genuinely required his attention by asking critical questions. If they didn't, I knew where to redirect them. Having confidence provides the courage needed to respectfully push back or redirect requests instead of automatically agreeing to every demand. Mastering this skill not only boosted my confidence but also assures those I support that I understand their needs and can be trusted to execute tasks appropriately.

The speed at which we develop confidence varies greatly from person to person, but if we think with a growth mindset, we can rest assured that confidence will develop as we become subject matter experts.

This is particularly true when it comes to mastering a new skill. If you have a few years under your belt as an administrative professional, I'm sure there are areas where you feel confident even if you don't realize it. Maybe you can easily juggle planning numerous meetings or manage calendars with ease. Here's the thing: you likely didn't feel as confident managing that task the first time you performed it. Your experience in repeatedly performing and ultimately mastering that skill has contributed to building your confidence in that area.

"I joined a new team in 2021 which utilizes a lot of vendors.," said one assistant. "You have to set up new vendors in the accounts payable system in order to pay them. In my previous role, I was okay with paying vendors, and I managed to make do, but now, setting them up was like a whole new challenge. What I find with confidence is that education and knowledge help build it. I really swam upstream with it and looking back, I wish that I could have helped myself a little bit more, but I learned a lot, including who I needed to talk to. I didn't really have anybody pointing me in any direction. But now, I'm like a subject matter expert. After coming through that whole learning process, I could set up a vendor in one day if I needed to because of everything I had learned."

Remember, as you build your confidence, you must be courageous in your approach. So many assistants I have encountered have been afraid of making a mistake that they are scared to make decisions. This fear of making an incorrect decision can result in constant reliance on asking others they perceive as more knowledgeable for guidance. While it is important to seek guidance when you truly need it, as a leader in the administrative space, it is crucial to also be able to confidently make decisions and understand that sometimes mistakes happen in the process. Perfection is not always attainable, but taking the initiative to lead and make decisions is necessary.

"When I make a mistake, I apologize for it, but it's hard for me to move on and let it go," shared an administrative professional. "One of the executives said, 'It will be so much better for you if you really moved on. Because if not, you'll make more mistakes just because you haven't let it go. The rest of us have let it go, because there's so much that I have going on that I'm not going to remember what you did. You move on, you apologize, you fess up, we're good.' So, learning how to make the mistakes, but really move on and let it go, has been huge for me."

Another administrative professional shared, "A lot of times I hesitate over things that I really don't need to hesitate about because my leaders trust me. If I make a mistake, they redirect me. Don't take it personally, know that you just need to learn. If you've made a mistake, you take the guidance, and you apply that to the next time."

The more you practice operating confidently, the more confident you will become in your abilities. Initially, it might feel unfamiliar and uneasy, but with time, it will become second nature and seamlessly integrate into your work style and interactions.

EVOLUTIONARY EXERCISE

Use the following prompts to map out your strengths. Take your time to reflect and be honest with yourself.

Core Administrative Professional Skills

- List the core skills required to be an effective administrative professional in your role. For example, organization, time management, communication, problem solving, event planning, etc.

- Reflect on your performance in each of these core skills. Rate yourself on a scale of 1-10 (1 being the lowest, 10 being the highest) for each skill.

Your Individual Skills

- Review your ratings and identify the skills in which you have scored the highest. These are the areas where you excel and demonstrate exceptional abilities.

- Write down specific examples or instances where you have successfully utilized these skills. Highlight moments or projects where you demonstrated your strengths effectively.

- Consider feedback from colleagues, managers, or clients. Reflect on any positive feedback you have received regarding your performance.

Other Unique Abilities and Talents

- Think beyond the traditional administrative professional skills and consider your unique abilities and talents. These could be skills acquired from previous roles, hobbies, or personal interests.

- Identify any transferable skills that set you apart as an administrative professional. Examples could include event planning, social media management, data analysis, etc.

- Reflect on instances where you have utilized these unique abilities in your role. Note specific examples or projects where your unique skills have made a difference.

Future Development

- Based on your identified strengths, consider how you can further develop and refine these skills. Explore professional development opportunities or training programs to enhance your strengths.

- Consider how you can leverage your strengths to take on new responsibilities or advance your career. Consider ways to apply your strengths in different contexts or projects.

- Reflect on how your strengths align with your long-term career goals and aspirations. Consider how your strengths can contribute to your overall career growth and success.

By recognizing and capitalizing on your strengths, you can enhance your job satisfaction, performance, and overall professional growth as an administrative professional.

Strategic Partnership

As you cultivate your confidence and shift your perspective to view those you support as colleagues rather than superiors, you unlock the ability to adopt a partnership mindset. This mindset empowers you to proactively collaborate with your executives instead of merely waiting to be assigned tasks or responsibilities.

In the past, much of the role of an administrative assistant was task-based. The focus was on completing assigned tasks efficiently and effectively. However, as the business landscape evolves, there is a growing recognition of the need for administrative professionals to adopt a more strategic partnership mindset. One way to develop this is to look at the bigger picture and take a more holistic approach to providing support.

The concept of strategic partnership within the administrative profession has gained significant traction in recent years, and a wealth of information is available on how assistants can be more strategic in their work. Moving away from merely performing assigned tasks and instead adopting a targeted, proactive, and systematic approach to our responsibilities has become a more sought after behavior in assistants. Rather than being solely task-focused, those of us with a strategic partnership mindset become goal-focused, aligning our efforts with the broader objectives of our managers, organizations, and teams.

One way that I was able to be more strategic in my work was by identifying a need for process improvement and resource allocation. When the team of executive assistants I managed was initially created, it was decided that they would support vice president level executives with calendar management, meeting and event planning, and other special projects as assigned. Yet,

I knew there were others who sat in positions below the vice president level that would need administrative support as well. While we were not able to give them the level of dedicated support provided to the vice presidents, I created a shared services model that allowed anyone in the organization to place a request through a ticketing system to ask for temporary administrative support for special projects, meeting support, and other activities. Through this simple process, an employee could answer basic questions providing details of their administrative needs. I would then receive the form and allocate the assignment to someone on the administrative team based on capacity, bandwidth, and interest. This model proved to be a win-win for the business and the administrative team. It gave the team an opportunity to work on special projects in addition to their routine responsibilities while meeting the needs of the business stakeholders.

From my example, you can see that demonstrating a strategic partnership mindset does not always require a huge undertaking; the most important part is to develop the mindset itself. By implementing the following activities, you will begin to cultivate a strategic partnership mindset.

- Expand your knowledge base. Gain a deeper understanding of the business and your executives, managers or teams' vision, goals, and priorities. Pay attention, listen, and ask questions. Connect with others on the team and engage in cross-functional collaboration to significantly improve your understanding of the overall business context

- Boost your level of initiative. This builds on developing your confidence. Administrative professionals should feel comfortable making decisions, solving problems, and offering perspectives on matters that advance the business. This approach enables you to contribute to the organization's success and empowers you to be a driving force behind key initiatives.

- Pursue opportunities to increase your responsibilities. Take on new projects, spearhead initiatives, or assume leadership roles within teams. By expanding the scope of your work, you demonstrate your value and willingness to contribute to the organization's growth and success.

- Build strong relationships and networks. By forging connections with colleagues, stakeholders, and other professionals in the industry, administrative professionals can leverage these relationships when needed to facilitate business operations and achieve objectives. You become a valuable resource within the organization, capable of tapping into your network to overcome challenges and seize opportunities.

- Anticipate the needs of your teams and managers. Administrative professionals with a strategic partnership mindset are always one step ahead, looking "around the corner" to identify upcoming business needs and opportunities. By proactively preparing those you support for what lies ahead, you enable your teams to navigate challenges effectively.

Particularly for those of us who have supported the same executive or teams for a significant amount of time, being able to anticipate their needs becomes a true value add.

I worked with one assistant who knew that all the large employee meetings would take place quarterly. At the beginning of the year, she would map out the tentative dates and place holds on the calendars of the leaders of the organization and all the employees critical to the meeting's execution to include IT, assistants, and facilities. Weeks prior to each meeting, she would remind the leadership team of the upcoming meeting and prompt them to create their portion of the presentation, providing them with a submission deadline to submit their slides for review and ensure template consistency. She would also do rehearsal meetings with IT to ensure that all the AV equipment was working properly.

Not only was her attention to detail in managing the meetings impressive, but she also carried out all these tasks without being prompted. Instead, she anticipated the needs of her manager, and created and implemented a plan to meet them. Her manager was beyond grateful that the details were cared for and that he could just show up and present to the employees.

The ability to anticipate needs and provide support when not prompted is one of the most impactful ways you can add value. While it may take time to learn about the needs of those in your organization, look for instances to begin capitalizing on this approach, even if you are newer to your role.

Watch for roadblocks and explore possibilities. Work to find solutions even when it may appear that none exist. Explore alternative approaches, think creatively, and adapt to changing circumstances. Learn to identify potential roadblocks, anticipate challenges, and provide your teams with valuable information to inform their decision-making. By serving as a reliable source of insights and support, you can empower your organization's leaders to make informed choices and drive the business forward.

EVOLUTIONARY EXERCISE

Take the following action steps to develop your partnership mindset in each area.

Knowledge Base Expansion

- Identify one key area to expand your knowledge and understanding of the business and your executives, managers, or team's vision, goals, and priorities.

- List specific actions you can take to gain deeper insights into this area (e.g., attending relevant workshops or webinars, reading industry publications, scheduling meetings with key stakeholders).

- Implement at least one action from your list within the next week to expand your knowledge base.

Initiative Boost

- Reflect on a recent situation where you could have taken more initiative or offered your perspective to advance the business.

- Identify an area or project where you can proactively contribute and make a difference.

- Develop an action plan to take more initiative in this area, including specific steps you can take to provide proactive support and contribute to the success of the organization.

- Implement at least one action from your plan within the next month and evaluate its impact on your role and the organization.

Opportunity Pursuit

- Assess your current workload and identify one project or initiative where you can take on additional responsibilities.

- Discuss this opportunity with your manager or team members, highlighting how your increased involvement can benefit the project and the organization.

- Create a plan to manage the additional responsibilities effectively, considering potential challenges and resources required.

- Take proactive steps to gradually increase your involvement and contributions in the identified project or initiative.

Relationship and Network Building

- Identify three individuals within your organization or industry with whom you would like to build stronger relationships.

- Take the initiative to reach out to these individuals through professional networking events, virtual meetings, or email introductions.

- Actively engage in conversations, ask insightful questions, and seek opportunities for collaboration and mutual support.

- Regularly nurture these relationships by staying in touch, sharing relevant resources or information, and offering assistance when needed.

Anticipating Needs

- Reflect on your role as administrative professional and identify one specific task or responsibility where you can anticipate needs and add value beyond the immediate requirements.

- Develop a strategy or action plan to proactively address those needs and contribute to the overall success of your team or organization.

- Implement your strategy and monitor the impact of your proactive approach, noting any positive outcomes or feedback received.

Finding Challenges and Possibilities

- Identify one recent challenge or problem you encountered in your work.

- Brainstorm alternative approaches or creative solutions to overcome this challenge.

- Implement one of the alternative approaches or creative solutions and evaluate its effectiveness in resolving the challenge.

- Reflect on the lessons learned and develop a mindset of resourcefulness to approach future challenges.

Organizational Priorities

Understanding organizational priorities is essential to the Mindset principle. By gaining insights into your organization's priorities and understanding your team's key focus areas, you can concentrate, minimize distractions, and accurately identify the tasks that warrant top priority in your work.

As an example, during the height of the pandemic, one of the challenges that my organization's executives faced was that they were inundated with meetings. As a provider of home-based services like cable and internet, that industry is one that experienced increased activity during the pandemic spurred by heavier usage due to so many more people being at home. In addition, the number of decisions being made regarding our employee population created a heightened need for decision-makers to connect. And since everyone was working remotely, these meetings would run into the lunch hour and beyond traditional working hours. Our Human Resources department recognized there was a need to encourage teams to avoid scheduling meetings during the lunch hour to give employees an opportunity to eat and take a break. While it was vital that our executives address pressing organizational issues, it also remained a priority to support our teams in performing optimally by avoiding burnout. As someone leading a team of assistants, I instantly recognized how we could help to reinforce this priority. Since many of us were responsible for managing calendars and scheduling meetings, we could have a direct impact on this by avoiding that time. It was our way of being able to support the business initiative.

In order to understand your organization's priorities, it's important to develop a curious mind, an interest in expanding your knowledge, and the recognition that the more we know, the more effective we will be in providing administrative support. For example, imagine you are in your department's meetings, building your knowledge about the business, listening to conversations between your manager and their direct reports. After the meeting, you review your manager's calendar and notice that some of the topics discussed are related to upcoming events. With an understanding of the business, you can proactively contact the subject matter expert from the direct report team who addressed those topics in the meeting. This allows you to gather the necessary information and prepare your manager for future meetings. Developing this understanding can empower you to anticipate your leader's needs and provide valuable support.

Assistants should become keen observers of the executives and teams they support so they can better understand the executives' visions, the intricacies of team dynamics, and the subtle nuances of decision-making processes. Measures like taking notes on action items and absorbing the discussions, debates, and underlying currents of ideas can help bolster this understanding.

A fellow assistant who works for a large medical organization shared that one of the responsibilities of her role was to take meeting minutes and follow up on any deliverables that were discussed. In doing so, she learned that one of the team's concerns was the ineffectiveness of an automated system they used to contact patients. They needed to reach out to these individuals to get vital information, but through the answering service they were using to make the calls, they had a hard time getting people to answer the phone. Upon learning this, the assistant suggested that the organization find a VoIP company to make the calls so that they would appear to be coming from an easily recognizable local area code. She took the initiative to research a VoIP company, and as a result of the research and implementing the suggestion, there was a 67% increase in patients answering the calls.

By understanding the organization's priorities and taking the initiative to help solve challenges around them, she was able to help her team meet their goals and contribute greatly to her organization's success.

Another great way to understand your organization's priorities is to take advantage of opportunities to attend events or training and learn about the products and services offered by the company. For instance, if your company is launching new products, familiarize yourself with them and their importance to the business. This broader knowledge equips you to better comprehend what matters to your organization. Consequently, you can play your part in facilitating and advancing those important initiatives.

Documents prepared for meetings can also be valuable tools to give us insight into business priorities and projects. Since many of us routinely have these in our possession, we can use this knowledge as an opportunity to identify ways in which we can influence and support the execution of these projects.

This information can provide opportunities to make an impact.

- Ensure meetings for these topics are prioritized over others
- Understand who the key players are and make sure that they have what they need to execute
- Identify if there is something within our own scope to contribute

For example, through a document that came across my desk, I learned my executive and his leadership team were planning to have a meeting with a global company to discuss becoming partners on what would be a large initiative for both organizations. Understanding that this would be an important first meeting, I took the initiative to partner with our communications team to build a presentation that would include professional biographies for all attendees in the meeting to include their professional headshots and functional business responsibilities.

Using this document allowed me to understand my organization's priorities and then take the initiative on what ended up being something we could send in advance to the other company in preparation for the conversation.

Additional tactics could include attending shareholder meetings, following the company's social media accounts and setting up a Google alert for whenever your company is mentioned in the news. The best way to go about understanding your organization's priorities can vary based on your role and organization.

The following administrative professionals shared some of the different tactics they employ to stay informed:

"When I was in my assistant role, I really felt like any time I got to be in a meeting was an opportunity. Even though I was there taking notes to support the meeting, I was in there like a detective. It's such an honor to have a seat at those tables. And if you look at it with the mindset that, 'Yes, I'm here to take notes and to capture some action items. But I'm also here to connect the dots and to use this as context to understand what's going on in my company,' you can also view it as an opportunity."

"There are typical staff meetings that we participate in with our executives. But I've learned to step out of that realm and attend other meetings. I have weekly one-on-ones with a VP that reports to my executive because her team does a lot of cross-functional support throughout the organization, so it's just an opportunity for us to sync. Attend other meetings, even if you're just taking notes. That allows you to understand some of those acronyms that you always hear that you may not understand. You get a glimpse of what's a high-priority request, so that when an executive or direct report requests a meeting about those activities, you know the level of importance because you've sat in those other meetings. You understand that this is a hot topic at your organization, and you know how to prioritize it. Having that knowledge makes our job easier."

I work in financial services, so there are many different tiers to finance–the businesses are so complex. What I have found really useful are the PowerPoint decks that I need to print for client meetings. I read through those decks where they explain what the company does, what each department does, the names of individuals, and the acronyms, and I save those decks in my folders. That's where I learned a lot of what our business does."

EVOLUTIONARY EXERCISE

Use the following prompts to map out a process for identifying organizational priorities and learning about your company's offerings. Take your time to reflect and think critically about your company's context.

Identifying Organizational Priorities

Research and identify key sources for understanding your company's priorities. Consider sources such as strategic plans, annual reports, executive communications, or company presentations.

- List the departments or teams within your organization that play a significant role in shaping its priorities. Identify areas such as marketing, sales, operations, finance, or human resources.

- Reflect on your interactions and conversations with colleagues, managers, or leaders. Consider any discussions or guidance provided regarding the company's strategic focus.

Understanding Service and Product Offerings

- Review your company's website and marketing materials. Explore sections such as "Products," "Services," or "Solutions" to gain insights into what your company offers.

- Identify key customers or clients your company serves. Consider the industries, sectors, or target markets that your company caters to.

- Engage with relevant teams or colleagues involved in developing or delivering services or products. Seek conversations or meetings with individuals from departments like sales, product development, or customer service.

Mapping the Process

- Develop a step-by-step process for gathering information about your company's organizational priorities and offerings. Consider activities such as research, interviews, attending company meetings, or reviewing internal documentation.

- Outline specific questions to ask during conversations or interviews with colleagues. Examples: What are the company's top priorities for this year? How do our products/services contribute to the company's goals?

- Set aside dedicated time to learn and update your knowledge about your company. Schedule regular checkpoints to review and stay informed about any changes or updates.

Applying the Knowledge

- Reflect on how understanding your company's priorities and offerings can enhance your role as an administrative professional. Consider ways to support the company's goals and contribute to its success.

- Identify areas where you can align your tasks and responsibilities with the company's priorities. Look for opportunities to streamline processes, support initiatives, or suggest improvements.

- Consider how this knowledge can help you better assist the teams within your organization. Think about how you can offer valuable insights or support in achieving the company's objectives.

Review your responses and use this exercise as a roadmap for gathering information about your company's priorities and offerings. By understanding the organizational context and aligning your work accordingly, you can enhance your effectiveness as an administrative professional and contribute to the overall success of your company. Regularly revisit and update your knowledge to stay informed about any changes or developments within your organization.

Systems

A systems mindset means developing a working knowledge of the technology, tools, and systems that our organizations utilize to accomplish business objectives. If you currently harbor a fear of new technology and tools, it is important to overcome that fear and acquire a basic understanding, at minimum, of the technology and tools used within your organization to excel in your role. As I have mentioned and as you know, technology will continue to advance, and organizations will continue to adopt new developments, and if you choose not to advance along with your organization, you put yourself at risk of being left behind with overhead projectors and floppy disks!

A systems mindset improves your effectiveness and efficiency as an administrative professional. Operating with a systems mindset does not mean that you need to master every tool. However, having a working knowledge of the systems at your organization demonstrates your commitment to being competent and ensures that those you support can carry out their work seamlessly.

To foster a systems mindset, recall the lessons you've undertaken to cultivate a growth mindset. It's important to recognize that your current unfamiliarity with new technology or tools doesn't signify an inability to learn. Embrace opportunities like online courses or in-person trainings to expand your knowledge base. Seek guidance and support from colleagues more experienced in technological domains. Break down the learning process into manageable steps, dedicating regular practice sessions to each. Understand that mastery comes through focused learning, one step at a time.

Of course, each system you manage will be different, but the specifics of the systems don't matter the most– it's your mindset around managing them. The two keys to taking on any new system with confidence are being proactive in seeking knowledge and being committed to continuous learning.

An administrative professional works with a variety of systems.

- Computers and Laptops
- Enterprise Software
- Email Services
- VoIP and Unified Communications
- Collaboration Tools
- Cloud Services
- Database Management Systems
- Cybersecurity Tools
- Virtual Private Networks (VPNs)
- Project Management Software
- Document Management Systems
- Enterprise Social Networking
- Data Analytics and Business Intelligence Tools

- Remote Desktop Software

- Video Conferencing Equipment

...and the list goes on and on!

As an administrative professional, I've always believed in taking the initiative to learn new tools and systems that enhance my ability to support my team. One memorable instance was when our conference rooms were transitioned to Teams devices. Initially, navigating these new devices wasn't intuitive for users. Sensing the need for clarity, I snapped pictures of the screens, compiled them into a PowerPoint deck, and added explanatory notes detailing each screen's function. This document was then made available in the rooms, serving as a helpful guide for users. I shared this resource with fellow assistants to ensure consistency in support across the organization.

By familiarizing ourselves with these resources, understanding and mastering tools and systems, we enhance our own efficiency and become better equipped to support our teams, executives, and colleagues effectively.

Take initiative to learn how to effectively manage the systems and tools required for your job. Familiarize yourself with new technology rollouts or system updates. In many companies, IT personnel handle the implementation of technology and tools, and it's worthwhile to connect with someone in your IT department when new systems are introduced to request a basic overview and gain a functional understanding of the technology. Some companies offer organization-wide training for employees to learn how to use the new technology, and if such training is available, it's advisable to attend it instead of solely relying on the IT person.

Several resources are available to enhance your tech proficiency. With the vast information available on the internet today, you can find tutorials and guides on practically any subject, including technology usage. Platforms like YouTube and LinkedIn Learning offer extensive tutorials and courses on various software and tools. Many software providers, such as Adobe, provide free training modules. If free resources are limited, consider it an opportunity to advocate for training within your organization. Extend your network beyond your workplace; connecting with other administrative professionals in different organizations often yields valuable insights and resources for skill development.

While you may not be an IT expert, a basic understanding of technology and tools empowers you to be self-sufficient and resourceful. It allows you to troubleshoot minor technical issues independently, which can reduce your reliance on external support and limit disruptions in your team's workflow. From my own experience, there is nothing worse than having a tech issue and waiting on someone from IT to show up and flip a switch in a room full of executives waiting to begin a meeting.

Cultivating a systems mindset requires a commitment to ongoing learning. Technology and tools evolve rapidly; staying updated on advancements and best practices is essential. Dedicate time to explore new features, attend webinars or workshops, and engage with online communities or forums related to the tools you utilize.

One assistant shared her experience finding the confidence and support she needed to embrace a systems mindset: "The very first day working from home, our VP got the leadership group on a call and my camera was broken on my laptop. One of the first things he said during the meeting was 'All right, while we're going to be working from home, I want everyone's cameras on,' and I couldn't put mine on. I was fairly new, and only had about nine months with the team. I was too nervous to speak up and say, I don't know how to do it. So, it was just one of those things I had to figure out. That learning curve was new to me. The assistants used to have practice sessions when we knew we were going to be having a team meeting. We started learning about breakout rooms. We would get five of us on a call and just practice and ask questions while we were going through. There was a lot of trial and error, but we did it! We were very blessed with the fact that everyone understood that we were in a new way of working. And I think most people were very patient and supported us learning new skills to support them."

This level of independence and problem-solving ability significantly enhances your effectiveness and value as an administrative professional. Not only does this expand your skill set but also demonstrates your dedication to stay current and adapt to the evolving needs of your organization, as well as your commitment to excellence, competence, and ability to support your organization effectively.

EVOLUTIONARY EXERCISE

Take a moment to reflect on the ideas presented in this chapter about developing a systems mindset. Consider the following points.

- How comfortable are you with technology and the systems used within your organization? Reflect on any fears or hesitations and how they might hold you back from being more effective in your role.

- What steps can you take to overcome your fear of new technology and tools? Think about how you can proactively seek knowledge and acquire a basic understanding of the systems used in your organization.

- Are there specific systems or tools in your organization that you can focus on developing a deeper understanding of? Identify areas in which acquiring more knowledge and staying updated on advancements can enhance your performance and value.

Ownership vs. Employee

Next in your evolution is to shift from an employee mindset to an ownership mindset in your work.

Now, you may be thinking, "But I am an employee. Why would I develop a mindset to take ownership over something that isn't mine?" However, I want to reiterate; this evolution journey is not about your organization. It's about you. To effectively evolve, I ask you to consider moving away from simply thinking about yourself as an employee of XYZ organization to being the owner and operator of your career path.

These two distinct mindsets can significantly impact your approach to your overall success. The ownership and employee mindsets represent contrasting attitudes toward work, accountability, and personal growth.

Employee Mindset

An employee mindset reflects the conventional approach that most employees take concerning their work. They primarily focus on fulfilling their job responsibilities. The following characteristics typify the employee mindset:

- Conformity: Employees in the traditional employee mindset adhere to predefined roles and responsibilities. They may be reliable and committed to their work, but their primary objective is to meet expectations within their job descriptions. They may not actively seek opportunities to go beyond their assigned tasks.

- Risk Aversion: An employee mindset often tends to be risk averse. Individuals in this mindset prioritize stability and security, avoiding situations that involve taking risks or challenging the status quo. They may be more resistant to change and less likely to step outside their comfort zones.

- Working for Compensation: We all rightfully value financial compensation. Let's face it– regardless of mindset, we want to be fairly compensated for our work. However, employees operating with an employee mindset derive motivation solely from the financial reward. They do not seek fulfillment from the work itself and instead focus only on fulfilling their obligations in exchange for monetary benefits. They are much less likely to actively pursue personal and professional growth.

Ownership Mindset

An ownership mindset embodies the belief that individuals are accountable for the quality and outcomes of their work. It goes beyond fulfilling job descriptions and focuses on deeper engagement and understanding the broader purpose of one's job. The following key characteristics define the ownership mindset:

- Accountability and Responsibility: Those with an ownership mindset feel a deep sense of responsibility for their work. They recognize that their contributions directly impact the success of their executives, departments, and the overall business. This mindset extends beyond job descriptions, encouraging individuals to take ownership of their actions and outcomes.

- Flexibility and Dedication: Possessing an ownership mindset means being flexible with time and effort. Individuals willingly invest time and go the extra mile to achieve excellent results. They understand the importance of focusing on long-term goals and are committed to the success of those they support.

- Solution-Oriented Approach: Instead of complaining or seeking to pass on work to others, those with an ownership mindset actively seek solutions, take initiative, and embrace challenges. When faced with obstacles, they take risks and shoulder responsibility to find alternative paths to success.

Let's take calendar management as an example since managing schedules and calendars is a common requirement for executive assistants. With an ownership mindset, an executive assistant would approach calendar management differently than one with an employee mindset.

To adopt an ownership mindset, you want to be dedicated, solution-oriented in your approach, understand the business of your executive, and be strategic in the way that you handle the calendar, take full responsibility, and resolve conflicts among competing priorities. I can recall an executive assistant I once worked with who fully embraced the ownership mindset when managing his executive's calendar. Without his executive asking, he sat down with her to gain an understanding of how she wanted to handle meetings on a weekly, monthly, and quarterly basis. For example, she wanted to have a biweekly one-on-one meeting with her eight direct reports. Once he understood this, the executive assistant arranged the calendar so that, in one week out of the month, every day at 10 o'clock would be a biweekly one-on-one with an individual. In the following week, every day at 10 o'clock would also be a biweekly one-on-one, so she'd have four in one week and four in another week, but the meetings would always be in that same time slot.

This allowed the executive to know that 10 o'clock time slot was reserved for one-on-ones. It also helped the assistant to build out a more structured schedule and cadence for meetings. The executive was now not just meeting with people at random times, but instead operating within a routine and a schedule that she could become comfortable with.

The assistant also learned that the executive had three monthly one-hour meetings. In response, for three of the four weeks, he blocked out those three monthly meetings on Thursdays at two o'clock. He would then hold that fourth Thursday for one hour at two o'clock, for any other monthly meetings that the executive wanted to add in that slot. He would keep a spreadsheet that he could always reference and know that if another monthly meeting were to arise, he had a slot to use. Using this method and color coding the spreadsheet helped to avoid conflicts and calendar collisions.

At the end of the year, he would revisit the schedule with the executive and talk about the meetings on the calendar. Because he had tracked them on the spreadsheet, it was easy to figure out which of those meetings they would continue into the next year and which they could repurpose, or which ones were no longer needed.

The ownership mindset guided how the assistant approached the work. He took the initiative, which created a rhythm that ultimately allowed the executive to understand her schedule. The value of an ownership mindset is demonstrated through its impact on the executive and how she can more effectively handle her business.

An ownership mindset fosters innovation and prompts employees to think creatively, suggest improvements, and contribute fresh ideas to their team and the company. It also drives individuals to go above and beyond their assigned tasks and take the initiative to seize opportunities, solve problems, and contribute to the overall success of their teams and the organization. This type of thinking enhances job satisfaction by facilitating a sense of purpose and fulfillment in one's work.

To shift to an Ownership Mindset

- Educate yourself about the business: Understand how your role aligns with the broader objectives of the organization. This involves actively seeking knowledge about the company's operations, goals, and industry landscape to better contribute to its success.

- Adopt a proactive approach: Taking initiative without waiting for directions is a hallmark of an ownership mindset. Being proactive in task execution and seeking ways to contribute to the organization's objectives without constant prompting demonstrates a sense of ownership.

- Set goals aligned with organizational objectives: Setting personal goals that support the company's objectives and periodically assessing performance is vital. Getting feedback for continuous progress toward these goals is a tool for personal and professional growth.

- Take full responsibility and accountability: Owning your tasks from inception to completion showcases an ownership mindset. Focusing on the details and ensuring high-quality work while being accountable for the outcomes reinforces a sense of responsibility.

- Be a problem solver: Embrace challenges and actively look for solutions rather than passively encountering them. Being proactive in finding effective solutions contributes to the success of the organization.

The effects of this mindset go far beyond displaying an increase in professional value to your organization. This change in your approach to work is one that you can take with you wherever you go and contribute to your own professional and personal success moving forward.

EVOLUTIONARY EXERCISE

Reflect on the following as it relates to your mindset.

- How would you describe your current mindset toward your work? Do you identify more with the employee mindset or the ownership mindset?

- Are there any specific areas where you feel you can benefit from embracing an ownership mindset? Identify situations or tasks where taking ownership and proactive engagement could lead to better outcomes or personal fulfillment.

Concierge Approach

The concierge approach simplifies the lives of those we support but also enables us to showcase our own value and leadership. At its core, this practice emphasizes the delivery of outstanding service by embodying the role of what I like to call a **support leader**. As support leaders, our objective is to intentionally assist and serve our departments, executives, and teams in a manner that enables them to concentrate on their primary work responsibilities. In doing this, we enable those around us to focus on the tasks that truly matter and drive business success.

I call this the concierge approach because it is analogous to the work of a concierge at a hotel. A concierge manages various tasks. They arrange reservations, provide recommendations for things such as dining locations and happenings around town, all to enhance the guests' experience and make their stay more enjoyable. Similarly, as support leaders, we strive to anticipate needs, remove burdens, and create an environment where the individuals we serve can focus on their priorities and move the needle in their business.

For example, a personal assistant might schedule a daily block of time for their executive to eat lunch, read emails, and engage in other essential activities. Or they might have a cup of tea waiting for the manager who isn't feeling well or even text their manager at night to remind them of an early morning meeting. It's an approach that prioritizes service and ensures that the individuals we support don't have to worry about the smaller details.

"We had a VP from China visiting our New York office for the first time," one administrative professional told me, "And I set up about 20 meet and greets for her with all senior leaders. I went through the floor plans and took screenshots of where everybody's offices were and how to get there. I put them in all the meeting invites to try and give her an idea of where she was going. I was there for her when she needed me."

"If my executive is traveling, I always make sure that he knows what the weather's going to be. If he's going to a restaurant, I make sure he knows about the restaurant. If he's meeting with external executives, I will go to their LinkedIn and pull-down information about them to give to him ahead of time. Those are some things that I just do on a typical basis for him that are maybe a little extra."

Here's how you can apply the concierge approach in your work.

- Prioritize what matters: Your primary focus should be helping executives and teams zero in on what truly drives organizational success. By aligning your efforts with what's most important, you ensure that your support makes a real difference.

- Effective communication and problem-solving: Think of communication as your secret weapon. By mastering the art of understanding issues and bridging gaps, you keep everything running smoothly. Your role is to ensure that tasks and projects flow seamlessly, removing obstacles before they hinder progress.

- Listen, understand, and empathize: Active listening is crucial. By tuning in to the needs, motivations, and perspectives of your colleagues and executives, you build stronger relationships and establish trust. When they know you get them, your support becomes much more valuable.

- Ask the right questions: Precision in your support comes from asking insightful questions. Gather all relevant information to tailor your efforts effectively, ensuring that your actions align closely with the desired outcomes. The more you understand, the better you can target your support to hit the mark every time.

- Elevate the support experience: Your goal is to not just meet expectations but to exceed them. Look for little ways to make the experience better for those you support—whether it's providing helpful resources, solving recurring issues before they're even mentioned, or surprising them with a thoughtful gesture.

Implement these tactics and observe the impact it has on the productivity and satisfaction of those you assist. Maybe you'll find that your executive is able to focus more on big-picture strategies because you've taken care of the details. Or perhaps your team members feel less stressed and more motivated because you've smoothed out the rough spots in their day. The small adjustments you make can have a big ripple effect, transforming the way your team operates and how they feel about their work. And that's the true impact of being an exceptional administrative professional.

EVOLUTIONARY EXERCISE

Prioritization of What Matters

- Take a moment to reflect on the core objectives and priorities of the individuals or teams you support.

- Identify one specific task or process that you can streamline or make more efficient to help them focus on their essential business matters.

- Implement the improvement and observe how it positively impacts their ability to concentrate on their key responsibilities.

Effective Communication and Problem-Solving

- Choose a recent situation where you encountered a communication gap or problem in your work.

- Reflect on how it could have been handled more effectively. Consider alternative communication strategies or problem-solving approaches that could have led to a better outcome.

- Apply these strategies to a similar situation in the future and assess the impact on the smooth running of tasks and projects.

Active Listening, Comprehension, and Empathy

- Practice active listening by selecting a colleague, executive, or client and engaging in a conversation with them. Focus on fully understanding their needs, concerns, and goals.

- Ask clarifying questions and take notes to enhance your comprehension.

- Pay attention to nonverbal cues such as body language, facial expressions, and tone of voice. These subtle signals often convey emotions and sentiments that words alone may not express.

- Empathize with their perspective. Put yourself in their shoes and genuinely strive to understand their thoughts, feelings, and concerns. This fosters trust and encourages open communication

- When the conversation is over, reflect on their motivations and perspectives, and identify ways you can respond to meet or exceed their expectations.

Ask the Right Questions

- Think of a task or project you are currently working on or will be working on soon.

- Before you execute, write down a set of relevant and targeted questions that will help you gather all the necessary information.

- Delve deeper into each aspect of the task or project and seek clarity.

- Use these questions as a guide to ensure precision and alignment with the desired outcomes.

Elevate the Support Experience

- Identify one area where you can proactively address a concern or improve the experience for the individuals you support. It could be providing resources or tools that enhance their productivity, anticipating and resolving a recurring issue, or surprising them with a thoughtful gesture that exceeds their expectations.

- Implement the action and observe the impact on their overall experience.

CHAPTER SUMMARY

- A fixed mindset can be transformed into a more rewarding growth mindset by implementing the right tools and strategies, fostering continuous growth, resilience, and personal development.

- Confidence in an administrative professional's journey to success is vital, and it can be undermined by the belief that executives know more. To build confidence, recognize your unique expertise, hone your skills, be well-informed about those you support, make decisions, and embrace challenges with a growth mindset.

- A strategic partnership mindset empowers administrative professionals to proactively collaborate and align their efforts with organizational objectives.

- Understanding organizational priorities involves gaining insights into your organization's goals and key focus areas to bring the best value to your role. Developing an understanding of the business and its priorities allows you to concentrate on essential tasks, eliminate distractions, and anticipate your manager's needs.

- A systems mindset involves acquiring a working knowledge of the technology and tools used in the organization to improve effectiveness and efficiency as an administrative professional.

- Shifting from an employee mindset to an ownership mindset involves taking accountability for the quality and outcomes of one's work, going beyond job descriptions, and actively seeking solutions and improvements.

- Concierge approach entails becoming a support leader, focusing on providing outstanding service and allowing those we support to concentrate on essential tasks and business success.

Management

A TALE OF TWO ASSISTANTS

Despite having the ability to excel at some of her tasks as an assistant, Amanda struggled in the new work environment. Tasks like setting up in-person meetings and booking travel arrangements that used to take up so much of her day were no longer a part of her work. Her manager was more often managing his own calendar, so even that activity was minimized. In the meantime, she remained frustrated by the new technology and was slow to adapt to it. Instead of taking the initiative to find ways to learn more, she instead waited for her manager to direct her to do more traditional tasks, which were becoming less and less necessary as time progressed. She began to spend most of her time scheduling events her manager wanted to be added to the calendar, setting up virtual meetings, and responding to emails without venturing beyond these tasks.

On the other hand, armed with her new mindset strategies, Tanya saw the remote work situation as a chance for reinvention and believed that this was an ideal moment to showcase her untapped skills and potential. She recognized that she could gain valuable insights into the business objectives and goals by actively engaging with her manager and the team. With this knowledge, she would be better equipped to provide exceptional support.

While she still struggled with confidence and being willing to speak up, Tanya stepped out of her comfort zone and began reaching out to her manager and team members, expressing her interest in joining various business meetings. She explained the benefits of her participation, including the fact that by participating in meetings, she could better understand the needs of those she supported, and emphasized her commitment to understanding the organization better. Her proactive approach surprised her manager and colleagues, who had yet to realize the depth of her skills and capabilities.

Motivated by her newfound confidence, Tanya took further steps to enhance her effectiveness. She enrolled in online courses and training programs to develop her skill set. Tanya implemented new processes and techniques to manage her and her team's time more efficiently. Additionally, she dedicated time to reading and learning about her organization and the industry in which she worked.

Tanya's determination extended beyond self-improvement. She actively networked with other assistants within and outside the company, seeking to learn and implement best practices in the evolving working environment. Through these connections, she gained valuable insights and guidance, strengthening her ability to successfully navigate the remote work landscape.

As time went on, Tanya's efforts paid off. Her manager and colleagues recognized her as an asset who consistently went above and beyond the scope of what was considered the traditional administrative role. Her team admired her knowledge, proactive approach, and dedication to professional growth. Tanya's transformation inspired others to follow suit, and a sense of camaraderie and adaptability spread among the assistants.

In contrast, Amanda's reluctance to embrace change and develop an Evolved Assistant mindset hindered her progress. She remained confined to her comfort zone. Amanda's failure to adapt and evolve in the remote work environment became evident. Her limited scope of responsibilities prevented her from showcasing her true potential, and her manager and colleagues gradually began seeking support from other assistants who had embraced the evolving role

---

Now that you've worked through developing the mindset of an Evolved Assistant, it's time to put it into action through the Management principle.

Management is where you take control of your behavior and begin to implement your new mindset. Through Management, you will gain valuable insights into your industry, current role, and desired future roles. This phase empowers you to sharpen your tools, seize opportunities to elevate your performance in your position, and apply your knowledge effectively. This is when you showcase your skills by taking tasks to the next level and showing your organization what you're made of. Management is all about super vision. When you master Management, you oversee your actions with a keen eye for improvement and quality. You conduct your tasks with precision, minimize errors, and step up your game to show everyone what it means to be a master of your craft.

Management is also about more than just executing tasks. It's about embracing the power of lifelong learning. Through Management, you embark on a journey of seeking and absorbing knowledge and becoming a powerhouse of expertise. You dive deep into your leader's and organization's goals and objectives, becoming full of industry knowledge in order to constantly stay ahead of the game. Here, you invest your time and resources into your professional development, to increase your knowledge about your position and to stay on top of your game.

When you master Management, you sharpen your tools, and you recognize and seize opportunities to learn new things and improve your existing skills. This is your time to embrace growth and development, apply what you learn, and test your results. Once you take the steps toward mastering this principle, you will be able to celebrate as your professional life blossoms.

There's a lot to learn here, so I want to reiterate that you should take your time! This evolution is not something you can rush through and see results. Read and reflect. Implement the lessons learned. Test your results and see how those small changes impact your work. And be patient! When you continue to take steps forward, you will find that those little changes pave the way for tremendous success.

Are you ready? Let's jump into the first section of the Management principle: Project Management.

Project Management

As an administrative professional, you possess a unique opportunity to approach your work through the lens of project management. This doesn't require you to become a certified project management expert or hold a Project Management Professional credential. Instead, you can tap into your own structured and strategic way of thinking to take your work to the next level and excel in your role.

When a task lands on your desk, instead of immediately moving ahead to execute it, take a breath and put on your project management hat. A running joke between me and my former team was that I would often tell them to "slow down gunpowder." As assistants, we are in the practice and habit of immediately executing on an ask, that we sometimes jump into action without thinking through the larger contextual impacts. So, I would encourage them and you to step back, think less about the small details, consider a wider perspective, and ask yourself these important questions: What are the objectives? What are the milestones and deadlines? What resources are required? Are there any dependencies or risks to consider?

Adopting this project management lens gives you a comprehensive understanding of the task at hand. You don't just execute mindlessly; you see beyond the surface and understand how each assignment fits into the larger strategy or objective. This shift in perspective empowers you to work more strategically and identify areas where you can optimize efficiency and enhance outcomes.

Approaching your work as a mini project is also an incredible opportunity for personal growth and expertise development. For example, suppose you're tasked with organizing a team meeting. Instead of merely focusing on scheduling and logistics, consider the broader context. Are there any critical objectives or deliverables associated with this meeting? What information or resources do the attendees require? How can you streamline the meeting agenda to maximize productivity?

When applying a project management perspective to meeting planning, you're thinking about factors such as scheduling, effective communication with attendees, and coordination with meeting owners. You're considering what deliverables are needed for the meeting to be successful. You're balancing costs and budget, setting deadlines and goals, and anticipating potential roadblocks to address them head-on.

I remember being given the task of orchestrating the logistics for not one, not two, but three executive meetings back-to-back, with the added twist of overlapping attendees traveling from multiple cities over a four-day period, meeting and staying in a large hotel. While I initially thought this was a good idea – kill two birds with one stone, as they say, I soon realized that the challenge of pulling this off would be daunting, and I knew I would have to rely on some core project management tactics and a bit of determination to conquer it.

The first was meticulous planning. I met with each executive to understand their goals, expectations, and preferred outcomes. Armed with a spreadsheet, I began to identify the key logistical details like meeting start and stop times, travel requirements and restrictions, catering preferences, audio-visual needs, team-building activities, and swag selections, to name a few.

Second, I had to consider resource allocation, specifically as it related to getting support from other assistants and hotel personnel. There was no way I would be able to do this alone, so I had to consider who I could employ to help me execute.

To further optimize the use of resources, I employed the third tactic: contingency planning. I reviewed every detail, anticipating potential issues that could arise during the meetings. From technical glitches to dietary restrictions, I had contingency plans in place for every conceivable hiccup. This allowed me to tackle challenges swiftly, keeping the executives' experience seamless and stress-free, which is always the goal.

As the meetings approached, the fourth principle, communication, became paramount. I maintained constant contact with all stakeholders, sending out regular updates, schedules, and reminders.

Shuffling 300 executives in and out of meeting rooms and keeping them on task required a lot of clear communication to ensure that everyone was on the same page and had the information they needed to participate effectively. The final and most crucial principle I adhered to was adaptability. The meetings were like a grand puzzle, with each piece constantly shifting. Attendees came and went, unforeseen issues cropped up, and schedules needed adjusting. Flexibility was my ally as I juggled these moving parts, making on-the-fly decisions to keep everything running smoothly

Adopting the fundamentals of project management adds structure to your daily work, helping to clarify priorities and enable precise allocation of time and resources. This practice enhances your ability to anticipate and address challenges, identify risks, and manage dependencies from the outset, ensuring successful outcomes. Integrating project management into administrative tasks is a game-changer, enhancing work quality, fostering personal growth, and facilitating expertise development. By thoroughly analyzing task components, routine assignments evolve into strategic opportunities. And while embracing this approach may initially seem time-consuming, especially for busy administrative professionals, the upfront planning pays off in the long run. It allows you to visualize project trajectories, foresee potential bottlenecks, and organize tasks efficiently, ultimately saving time by preventing errors or delays. This foresight minimizes the need for corrective measures during task execution, optimizing productivity and workflow.

Over time, successful performance allows you to build a reputation for yourself as someone who is knowledgeable about a particular task or project, and you begin to position yourself as a subject matter expert.

A Sharper Toolkit

Have you ever truly taken the time to sit down and assess your strengths and weaknesses?

Many of us have a general idea of where we shine and where we stumble, and often this loose knowledge is gained through trial and error and influenced by some vague sense of what we like to do and the tasks we take part in often. However, to take charge of our professional growth, it's time to pinpoint those areas accurately through self-assessments.

Take a moment to embrace this truth: **the areas where you need improvement are not hidden. Even if you can't see your gaps, the people you support likely can, so it's important to identify and address them head-on.** We need to recognize our strengths and weaknesses and find ways to enhance our effectiveness.

Fortunately, there are plenty of external opportunities for skill development, even if our organizations lack specific training programs for administrative professionals. A platform like LinkedIn, for instance, is a gold mine. Connecting with other administrative professionals on the platform is one way to learn about what opportunities exist for training and development, and it also includes information about training resources and free courses that can support our professional growth. Soft skills training, in particular, is highly valuable. For instance, if communication poses a challenge for you due to differing communication styles between you and your manager or team members, there are countless trainings and research materials to help you navigate different communication styles. Executives and successful professionals, regardless of their specific field, often invest in communication training, so we should not take this off the table for ourselves.

Take, for example, an executive assistant I know who had a major struggle with communication style. Her emails confused her manager, leading him to seek clarification from anyone in the office except her, creating an inefficient and frustrating way of working with one another. Realizing the breakdown in communication between her and her manager, she discussed her frustrations with a mentor who guided her toward a short professional development training on communications styles. After taking the course, she felt empowered to schedule a one-on-one meeting with her manager, expressing her eagerness to improve their workflow.

During the meeting, the assistant openly discussed the issues with email communication and expressed her desire to enhance clarity in her messages. Together, they devised a strategy to ensure effective communication, which involved the assistant summarizing key points at the beginning of her emails and using bullet points to highlight important information.

The assistant also asked for feedback regularly to ensure that her communication was meeting the manager's expectations. To foster better understanding, they agreed upon a set of guidelines for email correspondence and established regular check-ins to discuss ongoing tasks and projects.

As a result, the communication breakdown was addressed, leading to a more efficient and collaborative working relationship between the assistant and her manager. Doing this significantly reduced misunderstandings and created a more productive work environment for both parties.

In addition to LinkedIn, YouTube is also like a virtual tutor at your fingertips, providing tutorials on everything from Microsoft Teams tips and tricks to communication skills and emotional intelligence. Well-known online assessments, like the Myers-Briggs Type Indicator (MBTI), can help individuals understand how they perceive the world, make decisions, and interact with others, while tools like CliftonStrengths identify top strengths for leveraging natural talents in personal and professional growth. Exploring these platforms is a great way to initiate your journey towards up-skilling.

We also have a world of resources that cater specifically to our community through books, podcasts, and other materials focused on sharpening administrative skills. View the resources guide at the end of this book to find additional valuable sources of information to help guide you in your career.

The benefits of company-sponsored training are real, but while many of us see other employees taking advantage of it, we are often left out. But before you decide that it isn't available for you, have you ever considered asking if you could participate? Sometimes we don't get training because we don't ask.

Take my experience: I worked for an executive who had planned self-awareness training to help her team better understand themselves, gain insights into others, and optimize their workplace relationships. I asked if I could participate, and she said yes! I walked away from that experience with a greater understanding of myself and my communication style. Even more impactful was learning about how to communicate with others with differing styles. That training has been so valuable for me as I have moved throughout my career. So again, the message to you is this: if you hear of training within your organization, raise your hand to participate. You never know when the answer will be yes.

As you pursue more opportunities to learn, you may experience some pushback from others. This is definitely not something that always happens. Ideally, you work in an environment where those around you are supportive of your professional goals. However, if you do end up in a situation where colleagues are less than supportive, remember the perceptions we talked about earlier. There have been moments when I have faced instances where someone may have felt that I was undeserving of an opportunity either because of my role or because it was not something they had pursued themselves or was available to them.

I recall an instance when an executive I supported was taking his direct reports, which included me, out of the country for an international meeting. Before taking the trip, I was tasked with communicating to a few other departments that we would be out of the country, along with some travel needs necessary to ensure we could conduct business remotely. Sure enough, a director from one of the other departments made a trip to my desk right after receiving the email. "You're going with them?" he questioned, surprised that I would be among those selected to make the trip. The energy he projected my way was as if I should not have been invited to attend. I have run into situations like this many times over the years. You may also have your own war stories. Just use these encounters as a reminder that what someone else deems you worthy of has no bearing on what is actually true. Know that opportunities are just as open to you as they are to anyone, be willing to pursue them, and stand confident when you receive those advantages that you deserve.

Let me reiterate what I have said throughout this book from the beginning: this evolution is about you. It is wonderful if your organization provides you with the opportunity to sharpen your skills, but you will often need to take matters into your own hands to find the resources yourself. Don't allow your career path to be defined by what your organization does or does not provide. Understand your areas of growth and address them to take control of your own future success.

Time and Calendar Management

Time management isn't just about keeping track of minutes and hours; it's about taking control and maximizing time to make a major impact on the work of those you support.

Regardless of your role at an organization, you can benefit from understanding time management and scheduling. Time management is both theoretical and practical as it involves understanding and applying the principles related to effectively utilizing your time. At the theoretical level, time management encompasses ideas like prioritization, goal setting, task delegation, procrastination avoidance, and the psychology of productivity. Whether you are an executive assistant, scheduler, or working in a different administrative capacity, grasping these essential time management skills will undoubtedly enhance your effectiveness in your role as an administrative professional.

When you manage time effectively, you create space for your executive to focus on the high-impact business tasks. You become the guardian of their precious time, taking things off their plate so they can shine where it matters most. Mastering this helps you stand out from the crowd and allows you to have a significant influence over your executive's productivity.

I recall a conversation I had with an executive before I began conducting interviews to hire an executive assistant that would report to her. The executive talked about decision-making and referenced Steve Jobs wearing the same clothes to work every day because it was one less decision in a world where he constantly had to make many. The executive said, "We make so many decisions in a day. And if I can have an assistant come on board, who is able to make decisions, not as if they were an extension of me, but as if they were me, that becomes invaluable because it's one less decision that I have to make in my day and can make a huge impact on how I am spending my time."

Now, getting to a place where you feel comfortable making decisions as though you were someone else is not instantaneous. It takes time to get to know those you support and prove through your actions that you are skilled enough to operate on their behalf, so they entrust you with making those decisions. Once you build this type of relationship and are able to make these decisions with confidence, however, you become an invaluable asset to your executive's team.

I remember one of my executives wanting to organize a large off-site event for our employees. He charged me with bringing together all the functional groups to include HR, communications, facilities, and more into a meeting to discuss how we would pull off the outing. My executive had other pressing priorities at the time and entrusted me with being able to make decisions about the event without him being present. As the meeting progressed, and we worked through the logistics of food, giveaways, and activities, I acted on my executive's behalf, consistently giving feedback, and making the decisions I knew he would want to make. At some point, one of the department directors began to question my input. "Maybe we need to have this conversation with the executive," he continued to say. However, I was confident enough with the fact that I knew how to make decisions as though I were my executive that I stood firm in what I knew he desired. The department director continued to push until I included my executive in the conversation to get his input. As I knew, his answer remained the same as the one I had given. Even when questioned, I knew that my executive saw me as his representative and could rely on me to make decisions as though I were him.

So, how do you make decisions as though you were someone else? An Evolved Assistant needs to approach this thoughtfully and holistically. First you must pay attention. Study the executive you support. Listen to the way they communicate with others and pay attention to the way they respond in emails, for example. Take notes when you are in meetings with them so that you can learn to speak in their voice. Understand their preferences, priorities, and overall vision and consider these when making decisions about the calendar.

Think back to the Mindset principle when we discussed confidence and understanding your organization's priorities. Sometimes, assistants take a tentative approach to decision-making because they lack confidence, but confidence comes from understanding. Take the time to truly grasp what's happening around you. Approach managing time as a fact-finding mission. Don't be afraid to ask questions, whether it's to your manager or team members. Find out what meetings are about, why they're important, and if they align with your team's priorities. By having a deep knowledge of the priorities of your team, executive, or manager, you are then empowered to make decisions about managing time that reflect those priorities.

Once you have this understanding, you can make informed decisions about where your executive is spending their time and can adjust the calendar in a way that optimizes their productivity. A strategic assistant knows the optimal sequence of meetings, recognizing which ones should take priority. For instance, if you're supporting an executive, recognize the meetings they don't necessarily have to attend, and encourage their direct reports to step up and report back. Being aware of who can represent executives in meetings is crucial for seamless operations.

"Knowing organizational priorities helps me to be smarter as I am managing the calendar, because my executive doesn't need to be in a lot of those meetings," said one executive assistant. "I can then pull another person into the meeting instead and allow them to brief my executive during their one-on-one instead of putting it on his calendar."

Additionally, building in time for your executive to perform essential tasks like managing emails, lunch, bathroom breaks, and uninterrupted work is vital for maintaining productivity and focus. I've seen firsthand that mastering the calendar, as it directly impacts how an executive spends their time, is the key to becoming indispensable in this role.

For example, in my former role, if my executive had his all-hands meetings on a certain day at one o'clock, I would not let anyone on the calendar before one o'clock that day. The only way somebody could get in that time slot is if he would tell me he needed to connect with that person prior to the one o'clock meeting. I managed the schedule to align with his priorities and needs on that day. In my current role I support an executive who travels 70-80% of the time. She has a large direct report team, attends industry conferences, participates in speaking engagements, and in some ways is the "face" of the organization. My first thought upon seeing her calendar was that she was overscheduled. She had back-to-back meetings with very few breaks in between. There was no time for her to review emails, get from one meeting location to the next, think, or even take bio breaks. In my experience, I have never met someone who can perform their best with a schedule like this. Scheduling an executive's meetings back-to-back all day without any time in between shows a lack of understanding of how to manage the calendar and the executive's priorities.

Administrative professionals have many options to effectively manage time and calendars.

- Blocking out focus time on the calendar if an executive needs it.

- Building in break and travel times to their schedule.

- Noting why a meeting is being declined rather than simply declining it.

- Ensuring that teams know that anything that needs to be scheduled with an executive should come through the assistant.

- Asking for details, context, and an agenda when someone is inquiring about time on an executive's calendar

- Viewing the executive's calendar well in advance and resolving any conflicts

- Scheduling meetings for no longer than two-hour blocks of time so that executives are not in meetings for long stretches.

- Managing personal appointments as well as business meetings to minimize conflicts.

- Being constantly aware of what is on the schedule a month in advance.

- Building strategic time meeting blocks for months or even a year out to automate some of the calendar decision-making.

- Color coding meetings so that she can determine their level of importance at-a-glance

- Instead of creating 30, 45, or 60-minute meetings due to ease of scheduling, schedule 15, 20, or 25 minute-meetings, accounting for and building in time before and after the actual meeting time.

Not only does mastering the calendar showcase your talent, but it also helps make life easier for you. When you show your competence in managing time and schedules, you'll start to loosen the grip of some of the leaders who are afraid to relinquish control. They'll see that you've got this, and that they can trust you.

I once supported a Chief Financial Officer, and when I first saw her calendar, I couldn't help but think, "There's no way you can possibly do all of this!" She had double and triple bookings and meetings all over the place and was unnecessarily on calls with people from across the organization. I decided to thoroughly investigate the issue. I went to the CFO, sat her down, and printed out a month's worth of her calendar. We went through it day by day, meeting by meeting, and I asked about each one and why she felt she had to be there. She had seven or eight direct reports, and she wanted visibility, but if she didn't trust her VPs to handle their meetings, then she needed to reevaluate her organization.

She finally snapped out of it. It was like she had been waiting for someone to come along and have that conversation with her. But it took someone like me to feel confident and empowered enough to say, "Listen up, we're fixing this, and you need to trust that we can make it better." We were going to delegate and empower the VPs she had put in place to step up and take charge, and if anything, crucial came out of those meetings, we'd make sure she got the report. The things she absolutely needed to be in the room for I guarded like a hawk, but she had to let go of everything else. Once she began to have confidence in me, she began to relax her hold on the calendar.

Calendar and schedule management is where the magic happens. Mastering this art is like a quick win and provides the perfect opportunity to make an immediate impact. As an administrative professional, it's important to realize that you can take control in this area. Even if managers initially resist, demonstrating how you can streamline their day and boost productivity will eventually lead them to appreciate your efforts. When you step in, assume responsibility, and alleviate some of the chaos, they'll gradually recognize the value of having decisions taken off their plate. Your ability to make decisions on their behalf not only builds back time in their day but also strengthens your position as a key asset and partner.

Stealth-Like Behavior

Some assistants have a knack for entering a space with a bang, demanding attention, and screaming for recognition. But there's a better way to make your mark without being a walking tornado of noise and questions that drive your team up the wall. It's time to let your work shine and speak for itself like a gentle force of nature—a blanket of snow, a shower of spring rain—quietly and effortlessly making its presence known.

Once, I worked with an assistant who always inserted herself in conversations and places where it wasn't appropriate, didn't make sense, and often felt awkward. She would even interrupt executives while they were speaking to one another. I will never forget the day she walked into a conference room right before a meeting was about to begin. I was there to quietly ensure the technology was working in the room, and the executives were engaged in small talk, but it was definitely business related. She decided to jump into the conversation with a comment not related to the business topic they were discussing or the meeting subject. Immediately, you could feel the energy shift in the room. It was as if everyone was taken aback by her remarks, and a silence came over the room. She developed a reputation of being intrusive, and sometimes disruptive, which ultimately overshadowed her overall work performance.

When you exhibit stealth-like behavior, your efficiency, attention to detail, ability to anticipate your team's needs, and delivery of results that exceed expectations will be enough to impress. You won't need to announce yourself or constantly seek validation.

Let me be clear: stealth-like behavior doesn't mean hiding in the shadows or being invisible. It means being strategic, deliberate, and purposeful in what you say and do. It involves observing, analyzing, and executing with precision. It includes being the silent powerhouse behind the scenes, making things happen seamlessly.

So, how can you embody the essence of stealth-like behavior? Well, part of it is remembering that while we always want to show up confident, we don't necessarily need to show up loud. Just as much as it is important to know when to speak up, it's just as important to recognize when to step back and give someone else the floor. Practicing stealth-like behavior also requires being a good observer. Taking a few moments to observe the environment when entering a space helps us better read the room before speaking or participating. Practice patience. We shouldn't drag our feet when it comes to expressing ourselves and sharing those burning ideas, but we also need to recognize that there are better times than others to have those conversations. For instance, we don't want to bring forth non-urgent concerns during a time when our teams or executives are busy putting out fires.

Finally, know that progress requires practice. It may take some time to find a middle ground, especially if you are still working through bolstering your confidence, and that's okay.

Remember, while being stealth-like is essential, it's also important to strike a balance. Communicate effectively with your executives, keeping them informed of important updates and progress. Be present when needed, but don't overwhelm your team with unnecessary engagement. Choose your moments to shine and make them count.

Boundaries

It's all too easy to fall into a cycle of constantly taking care of those we support, working long hours, and sacrificing our personal time. Often, when we do this, we find ourselves not able to focus on our own development and the other things that matter to us. But being good at your job does not mean constantly putting yourself last to be available to everyone else. It's time to reclaim your power and learn to set healthy boundaries.

Understand Why Boundaries Are Critical

To set boundaries is not about being rigid or unhelpful; it's about creating a balance that allows you to be effective in your role while prioritizing your own growth. It's teaching others how to treat you and establishing guardrails that define what is acceptable and what is not to guide others in their interactions with you. Part of your evolution is creating a shift in the way people work with you so that you can reclaim your time and redirect your focus toward tasks that matter for your career development.

Many of us tend to say yes to every request, and we often go above and beyond, even stepping outside the scope of our job description. But I want you to consider this: you are on a journey to advance in your career. Your continued efforts to try to be everything to everyone will stand in the way of being able to do the things you need to do to evolve. After all, how are you going to find the time to enhance your own skills if you spend all your time focused on assisting everyone else? When you don't set boundaries, it becomes too easy to give up on the things you need to do for your career.

We need to discern between genuinely necessary assistance and instances where we are unnecessarily enabling others' dependence on us. We don't need to accommodate every demand. We are not doormats, and we are not superheroes. We are professionals with limits. Within the journey of evolving, we need to release the notion that saying yes to everyone is required. We also need to recognize that setting boundaries is not selfish; it is a practice that helps us bring the focus back to ourselves so we can make the tasks that directly impact the people we support a priority.

There is power in setting boundaries. Boundaries are gentle but firm reminders. They create space for genuine connections and understanding in our work relationships. Asserting our limits is a form of self-care. Boundaries empower us to earn respect from others by showing respect for ourselves and are our secret allies that bring harmony to our relationships, work, and ourselves.

Without boundaries, we can find ourselves overwhelmed and operating in consistent chaos. This can make us susceptible to stress, anxiety, and burnout. We prevent ourselves from reaching our full potential and showing up as the best version of ourselves. We also confuse those we interact with by failing to be honest and direct, causing us to also be unfair to those around us. This is because failing to establish boundaries blurs lines of communication and expectation, leading to misunderstandings, and ultimately hindering productivity and collaboration.

Setting clear boundaries in the workplace provides a framework for colleagues to understand how to engage and collaborate with you efficiently. As they become acquainted with your preferences and working style, they can align their approach accordingly.

With boundaries in place, it becomes easier to take charge of your time and priorities, reducing the need for constant reactivity to others' demands. This empowerment enables you to concentrate on your work based on your schedule, rather than consistently adjusting to others' timelines.

Establish Boundaries With Those You Directly Support

Once you clearly understand your boundaries and the importance of having them, you need to establish them with those you directly support.

Determine for yourself where the line between appropriate support and excessive demands lies and communicate that to your manager. If you've allowed those you support to request things that make you uncomfortable, it sends a message that you will do whatever is asked of you, regardless of whether those requests are crossing the line. When you set and communicate your boundaries, you teach those you work for how to treat you. This not only enhances your work-life balance but also helps to shift the perception of your job, compelling others to regard you as a colleague and professional rather than a subordinate.

For example, I spoke with an assistant recently whose executive had a habit of texting her at five o'clock in the morning with tasks he wanted her to complete that day. The executive was simply running down the list of what needed to be accomplished and did not expect that she would perform the activities at that moment. Yet the early morning notifications were disruptive to the assistant, and she could not help feeling that he would likely not send texts at that time of day to colleagues that he viewed as peers. While she was in a support role for the executive, she felt that she deserved the same respect.

Once boundaries have been set, demonstrate that your manager can trust you to anticipate their needs and proactively address them, minimizing the need for boundaries to be crossed. For instance, if an executive constantly contacts you for travel-related information, remind them how you have always meticulously prepared travel folders and added travel details to their calendars well in advance. Assure them that you're always one step ahead and then gently remind them of the boundary you've established.

In those instances where boundaries have been crossed, you need to have a conversation. Frame the conversation in your mind, consider the key points you wish to address, and communicate your intentions assertively. Be specific. Offer examples where you felt boundaries were crossed and suggest alternative solutions; in this example, this might be suggesting ways to reduce contact outside of work hours unless it is a true emergency.

Now I would be willing to bet that many of you are reading this and thinking to yourself, my manager is not going to adhere to this request. But I say stand firm, be consistent, and steadfast in your efforts. There can be value in challenging them to really think about their ways of working with you, and you can consider asking for their suggestions on how making a shift like this could improve and/or enhance your working relationship. And you can also assure them that boundaries can be flexible and be modified when necessary and appropriate.

Define Boundaries With Your Colleagues

You may find that everyone seems to turn to you for support, even if your actual job only requires you to support one person! It's valuable to be viewed as a resource at your organization, but sharing your knowledge and experience is not the same as doing everything for everyone or being available to assist others 24/7. And when you are repeatedly asked how to put in tickets, request that you order the catering, or questioned about how to use a certain tool or software, it's definitely time to set some boundaries.

One of the best ways to successfully do this with your colleagues is by empowering them to be self-sufficient. Teach them "how to fish" instead of solely relying on you as a resource. Show them how to access (and save) links, documents, relevant websites, or other resources. Encourage them to take more ownership of their tasks and guide them towards finding solutions independently, which can reduce the burden on you. You're not just lightening your workload; you're helping promote your team member's development and growth and fostering a culture of self-reliance in your work environment.

This, my friends, is the one I struggled with most. For those of us who have had the experience of working in the same organization for a long time, you tend to develop many relationships across teams and departments, hold a great deal of institutional knowledge, and are viewed as a resource catch-all (or at least it feels that way). When this is your story, like it was for me, it can be difficult to draw the boundary line. On any given day, people would call on me for a variety of reasons, often that had nothing to do with my primary responsibilities. When I would get the phone call that started with, "hey can I pick your brain on something," or "I just want to know what you think the best approach is on," I knew I was venturing into territory that was taking me away from where my time and energy should be focused.

How I Knew It Was Time For Me To Set Boundaries

I would typically start my day by coming in, turning on my computer, popping in to connect with my executives, and then returning to my desk to review emails. Because I color-code my emails, I can usually get right in and start working on the pressing matters of the day, which I code with the color green. I am one of those who stays planted at my desk most of the day. With my workload, it was easy for me to get behind if I didn't stay ahead of it all.

Well, on one particular day, between people making impromptu stops at my desk and a multitude of requests coming via Teams during the first three hours, I realized that I had gotten nothing accomplished. I was under a deadline to complete a project, and these interruptions, most of which had no direct bearing on my primary responsibilities, had delayed me from completing the work for my executive.

My anxiety was high, and I felt myself on the verge of tears because I was overcome with such an overwhelming feeling of frustration. I was on the verge of burnout, and I knew I could not keep doing this. I would have to find relief.

But here's the real deal – at that time, I'd had more days like this than not, and the truth is that I had continued to operate with no boundaries for far too long, which is what led to such an intense reaction that day. I did not want to disappoint my colleagues and feared representing my executive poorly if I told people I could not assist them with whatever they needed.

But that day showed me that enough was enough, and I needed to implement changes if I were going to be able to remain productive in my role.

Some of the immediate strategies I employed were to create a status message on my Teams account that read, "If you are contacting me for scheduling purposes, please send me an email." I don't know about you, but the constant pinging of direct messages can feel incessant. They can be distracting and easily forgotten if you are focused on another task. Asking for an email, particularly when a scheduling request is involved allows me to get to it when my time permits. I would redirect emails intended for others. For example, I would often receive questions from colleagues across the business that should have been asked of another assistant. Instead of providing a response, I began to forward that to the appropriate assistant and let them take it from there. I got comfortable (even when it was a bit uncomfortable) saying no to demands on my time that would keep me away from my primary responsibilities. I no longer hesitated to say, "No, I am unable to attend this meeting but happen to send someone on my behalf." I had to get clear and be honest with myself about what I allowed to fester in my work life. I have always seen myself as an ambassador of sorts for my organization, and for many years, relished the fact that people saw me adding value in that way. But I had to learn to take a breath and redirect people. Being everything to everyone was no longer serving me as someone who was navigating my career with purpose. I had to reach back to those lessons I had learned long ago about confidence. As long as I continued to perform my role with excellence and exceed my executive's needs, I did not need to run myself ragged trying to accommodate others and worry about how I was perceived in their eyes.

You likely have and will continue to encounter situations where you need to reinforce your boundaries at work. To navigate these conversations requires professionalism and respect. Be polite but firm with your redirect when faced with requests outside your established boundaries. Offer alternative solutions or suggest resources that can help them address their needs. By doing this, you communicate the value of your time and expertise while staying focused on your goals.

EVOLUTIONARY EXERCISE

Take some time to reflect on your past experiences at work and identify moments when you felt overwhelmed, stressed, or undervalued due to a lack of boundaries.

Define Your Values

- Consider what matters most to you in your work life. Is it maintaining a healthy work-life balance, having uninterrupted focus time, or being respected for your expertise? Write down your top priorities and values.

Identify Boundaries

- Based on your priorities and values, pinpoint specific areas where you need to set boundaries. This could include time boundaries (e.g., no meetings during certain hours), communication boundaries (e.g., responding to non-urgent emails within 24 hours), or task boundaries (e.g., saying no to additional projects when your plate is full).

Communicate Boundaries

- Practice assertive communication by clearly and respectfully communicating your boundaries to your colleagues and managers. Use "I" statements to express your needs and expectations and offer alternatives or compromises when necessary.

Reinforce Boundaries

- Consistently reinforce your boundaries by sticking to them and addressing any violations promptly and assertively. Remember that setting and maintaining boundaries is an ongoing process, so be patient with yourself and others as you navigate this journey.

Reflect and Adjust

- Periodically reassess your boundaries to ensure they continue to align with your values and goals. Be open to adjusting them as needed based on changes in your workload, responsibilities, or personal circumstances.

CHAPTER SUMMARY

- Project management involves approaching your work with structure and strategy while keeping the bigger objectives in mind. Break down tasks into their essential components to conquer them and with each project-like assignment, sharpen your skills, broaden your knowledge, and contribute to the success of your organization.

- Sharpen your toolkit by evaluating your strengths and weaknesses, and actively seeking opportunities to develop and refine your skills.

- Mastering time management can have a huge impact on your organization. Having the confidence and understanding to make decisions about time management allows you to build trust and helps you retain control in your work environment.

- Stealth-like behavior means being strategic, deliberate, and purposeful in what you say and do. Embracing this strategy includes observing, analyzing, and executing with precision and being the silent powerhouse behind the scenes, making things happen seamlessly.

- Establish healthy boundaries to protect your time and energy. Boundaries enable us to focus on our career growth and prioritize the people we support. Recognize the line between appropriate support and excessive demands, have open conversations, and guide others toward independence so you can create a more balanced and fulfilling professional journey.

Marketing

A TALE OF TWO ASSISTANTS

Amanda seemed to be stuck in a time warp. As her colleagues grew increasingly frustrated at her reluctance to explore new possibilities, Amanda's manager encouraged her to talk to other administrative assistants for inspiration. She reached out to those in her network and engaged in conversations and learned about their innovative approaches and fresh perspectives. However, despite gathering valuable ideas, Amanda struggled to put them into practice. She would try a few strategies, but when they did not immediately work, she would lean back on her tried-and-true tactics. Her fixed mindset held her back, and without guidance on how to move forward, she found herself waiting for things to magically revert to the way they were.

On the other hand, Tanya continued to take charge of her own destiny. She recognized the importance of adaptability and growth in the face of change and decided to seize the opportunity to redefine herself and her role in the organization.

She enrolled in a company-sponsored course on personal branding. She dedicated herself to discovering her unique strengths, values, and aspirations. With a clear vision of her personal brand, Tanya embarked on a journey of self-improvement.

To gather diverse perspectives, Tanya assembled a personal board of directors. This group consisted of her manager, a respected leader in the organization, a fellow assistant she collaborated with closely, and a trustworthy colleague known for their honesty. Tanya scheduled individual meetings with each member to collect feedback on her performance and how she was perceived. These conversations were invaluable in guiding her personal growth and shaping her professional identity.

Tanya didn't stop there. She recognized the power of networking and actively sought opportunities to expand her connections. Joining an employee resource group, she immersed herself in a diverse community, offering her administrative skills to support their initiatives. By doing so, Tanya showcased her abilities beyond her regular assistant duties, building a reputation as a reliable and proactive team player.

Motivated by her fresh insight, Tanya took the brave step of discussing her career aspirations with her manager. She expressed her love for the assistant role but also articulated her desire to broaden her scope of work. With a well-thought-out plan, she detailed how she envisioned contributing more strategically to the organization. Her manager was impressed by her ambition and commitment, and they began exploring possibilities to align Tanya's goals with the company's needs.

In this third principle, we're talking about Marketing, and before you yawn and say, "That's not my thing," let me tell you why it should be.

Most employees do not consider marketing themselves at work. They believe that marketing is a task that should be left to advertising executives or colleagues in the marketing department. However, I'm here to emphasize that they have misunderstood the importance of self-marketing in the workplace.

In the business world, marketing refers to the activities that a company takes part in to promote the value of its products, services, or goods. As an Evolved Assistant, marketing takes on a different meaning.

Marketing as an Evolved Assistant is all about promoting yourself and shaping how your leaders, colleagues, and teammates see you and the value you bring to your organization. Marketing is also the principle where you will define your career goals, build relationships, and let the world know what you're aiming for. This will be the time to communicate your intentions, so the right people can support you on your journey and connect you with the career satisfaction you're after. Through marketing, you align the image you present to the world as an administrative professional with your true talents and capabilities, allowing you to highlight your strengths in an authentic way.

It's time to take charge of your own marketing. Don't let the word scare you off. Embrace it, own it, and watch how it can boost your career trajectory. Remember, even if you're not in the marketing department, marketing yourself should be at the top of your to-do list.

Now, let's jump into the first tactic in the Marketing principle: Defining your personal brand.

Personal Brand

Much like marketing, there hasn't always been a focus on assistants creating their personal brand. When personal brand comes to mind for most people, they think it applies to entrepreneurs or influencers, not those in the traditional workplace. But this couldn't be further from the truth.

That's because your personal brand isn't about how to build your own business and sell the trendiest product. Your personal brand is about creating a widely recognized and consistent perception of who you are, based on your experience, expertise, and impressive track record within your community, industry, or the vast marketplace. Or, more simply put, it's how others see you and what they say about you when you aren't in the room.

Before I go any further, I need you to let go of the idea that what other people think and say about you doesn't matter or that you can just do whatever you want and allow everyone else to fall in line. That's perfectly fine if career advancement does not matter to you. You can keep doing everything you're doing if you're content to stay where you are. But if you're looking to climb the career ladder and/or be seen as the go-to expert and one whose opinion is valued, then you need to learn how to make your personal brand shine.

Think about this: We are all in a unique position within our organizations, and this is true regardless of your role as an administrative professional. For those of us who provide direct support to a high-level leader, you are a member of your leader's team, and you need to see that as an asset to your professional development and growth. You have, in some cases, access to those individuals that not everyone does. You are in the position to both learn from the decision-makers and showcase your skills in front of those with a high level of influence. But sometimes, we don't even realize the power we possess. The opportunity to brand yourself as a support leader of those with organizational authority should not be overlooked. Rather than perceiving the position of an administrative or executive assistant as low-ranking, we should view ourselves as key players at our organizations with a direct line to its leaders that we can benefit from if we highlight our strengths accordingly. To do this effectively requires defining your personal brand.

When people think of you, do they think you're resourceful? Do they think you're knowledgeable or experienced? Do they believe that you provide an elevated customer or support experience or that you're an expert in a discipline or function? All those things help to contribute to your personal brand. If you are an administrative professional who has not spent any time thinking about it, this is your opportunity to do so.

Please note, creating a personal brand doesn't mean that you need to stop being yourself. I am myself wherever I go, and I've built success while being authentic to who I am. How others see us should be reflective of who we are. It is hard to keep up the facade of trying to create an inauthentic brand, and everyone else will see it, too. When it comes to my own brand, I have stayed true to myself, and those words of wisdom and lessons learned from my mother's guidance.

Instead of creating a fake brand based on what you think "sells," define your brand by tapping into your strengths and highlighting what makes you unique to your peers and colleagues. This is how you'll showcase your expertise and accomplishments and let your actions speak for themselves.

But how do you define your brand? One of the best places to start is to create a brand statement.

Ask Yourself

- What do I want to be known for?
- What are my strengths?
- What do people think about when they hear my name?
- What do I want people to think about me?
- What do I think about myself?

Once you answer, your next step is to take those answers and build a personal brand statement. Your personal brand statement captures who you are professionally in words to help guide your actions and others' perception of you. The goal is to succinctly showcase your unique value and contributions, spotlighting your core attributes and strengths.

One way that crafting the statement is broken down is by using the I help _____ do _____ format, meaning I help (fill in who you help) do (fill in what you help them do). For instance, here is my personal brand statement, which is a more fleshed-out version of the I help_____ do _____ format:

> I am an administrative professional who manages processes, procedures, projects, and people. I help organizations by strategically partnering with executives to provide daily solutions in managing their time and workload, which enables them to be more focused on business deliverables. I

am a problem solver, organization guru, and execution expert who also thrives on collaborating with other administrative professionals to foster their success.

From this statement, you can see where I use my strengths and the audience I serve to help guide what I convey as my unique brand.

So where do you use this after you create it? After all, unlike Coca-Cola, it's unlikely you will be creating commercials for yourself, but you'll certainly use it on your resumes, in interviews, when networking and within your LinkedIn profile. But it's true significance lies in its role as your guiding beacon. When you establish a clear vision of how you desire to be perceived within your workplace, you can align your behavior to match it. For instance, if you aim to be recognized as the administrative professional who empowers executives by efficiently managing their schedules, you prioritize excelling in that area, even amidst other responsibilities. Similarly, if you strive to enhance company morale as an administrative professional by organizing departmental events, you discern which aspects of your work require your additional dedication and effort.

Your personal brand serves as a mission statement that guides your actions with thoughtfulness and strategy. By clarifying your personal brand and aligning your activities with it, those in your vicinity will gradually recognize your distinctive qualities, enabling you to pave the way for new opportunities and shape the career you aspire to and rightfully deserve.

Personal Board of Directors

After establishing your brand statement, it becomes crucial to identify individuals who can hold you accountable for achieving your goals and provide support throughout your journey. You cannot get to true career fulfillment without the collaboration, encouragement, and support of others. This group makes up your Personal Board of Directors (PBD) - your ultimate squad of evolution champions.

The key here is trust and diversity. You want to choose those you feel comfortable confiding in who ideally occupy a variety of positions within and outside of your organization so they can provide you with multiple points of view. There are some caveats, however. I would not advise recruiting someone that is not affected in any way by your work. If they don't have any awareness of what your job entails, you're likely talking to the wrong person. Instead, you want a dynamic group of three to four people who bring different perspectives and are in closer view to the way your work. These individuals are your steadfast supporters, fully committed to helping you achieve your career goals. You want their support to be consistent and their feedback to be as real as it gets. So, be intentional, be specific, and choose wisely.

My PBD includes

- A C-suite executive

- A Human Resources executive

(I've known both of these people for over a decade)

- Two executives who work in other parts of the organization who have served as mentors over the years

- A former manager

- An administrative leader outside of the organization in which I work

- My best friend (who also happens to be a former colleague)

Keep in mind that members of your PBD can change over time. As you navigate the journey you will meet and build relationships with additional people who may be able to provide guidance. As your goals change, your PBD may as well. Be vigilant in choosing those you can trust and be flexible in making changes as needed.

Spend some time thinking about three or four individuals who will make up your dream team. Think about their strengths, diverse perspectives, and influence within and outside of your organization. These people will give you the feedback you need and help you identify any gaps that need filling.

Once you identify your board, it's time to approach them. Communicate that you're in a place where you're trying to evolve and specifically, change the way you approach and think about your career. Express to them that you are actively seeking supporters who can champion this journey along the way. Set up a time to meet or talk to them to get their feedback. It will be important that you do some homework beforehand and come up with a list of questions to ask each board member. The evolutionary exercise following this chapter provides some examples of questions to ask.

Be ready for whatever feedback comes your way, so prepare yourself for the possibility of being uncomfortable with what you hear. Remember, now is not the moment to overly react to comments. Recognize that the feedback you receive might not align precisely with your own perceptions of your strengths and weaknesses and appreciate that this can be a positive outcome. It is not unusual for us to have blind spots when it comes to our own professional gaps and abilities, which is why hearing from others who view you from a different perspective is important.

Once you get their answers, don't just nod, and move on. I encourage you to think critically about what you have heard. Look for patterns in the feedback you receive. Maybe three out of the four people affirmed something you believe about yourself, or maybe they pointed out something you hadn't yet considered. When you see those patterns, ask yourself, "What skills do I need to develop in my areas that require improvement?" How do I build upon and highlight my strengths?" Use their insights to ignite your growth, seal those gaps, and propel you to where you need to be.

For example, I once received feedback from a member of my PBD that I tend to come across as abrasive. I know that I am very direct, but it's never my intention to be rude or abrasive toward anyone. Still, everyone doesn't perceive what I'm saying in the way that I intend it. I took my board's feedback to heart and decided to take steps to improve.

I actively began to apply the training I had participated in as mentioned in the Sharpen Your Toolkit section of the book. Through this process, I discovered the value of adapting my communication style to fit different personalities and preferences. I learned to tailor my approach to specific individuals, considering their unique communication styles and sensitivities. It wasn't easy but I would tell myself with my inner voice, "Slow down and think of the best way to respond based on the audience." When it was someone I did not know, I would default to really focusing on what they were saying to me so that I could offer a response that would leave a positive impression. Learning to do this made my interactions better, and it helped me build stronger connections with colleagues and team members.

Another administrative assistant addresses being told she was timid at a new job.

"I really did not like being told I was timid and hearing that I gave off that impression actually made me a little bit upset. But I started to recognize that it was coming from a place of just being insecure about my place in the organization. I was new there. I didn't know everyone and there was a lot that I just didn't know. So, I took that feedback, and I grew my network. I got to know all the administrative and executive assistants a lot more. I also got to know people that weren't assistants, and the more I knew, the better I felt. Now I don't think anyone at my job would call me timid."

I have also had the pleasure of serving on the PBD for others throughout my career, and I recall an assistant reaching out to me because she was having a challenge with a new executive she was supporting. Like many of us may relate to, when you begin a new support relationship, one of the initial goals is to understand the executive's preferences and work style. She was no different. She was committed to her work and wanted to make decisions in the right way. Despite her dedication to performing well and making informed decisions, the problem she faced was that her executive frequently postponed or shortened their meetings, leaving her frustrated, questioning her effectiveness, and unsure of whether she as making an impact. She contacted me to seek guidance on how to make the executive prioritize communication with her.

"My executive doesn't make time for me" is a common theme in our world. As someone who has been there, I had some immediate thoughts for her to consider. I gave this advice: First, settle in and practice patience.

Supporting executives is not a one-size-fits-all game. Consider the idea that perhaps this executive has not previously had strong administrative support and may not see the value in what an assistant can add to their life. It may require you to be direct in communicating why these touch points with the two of you are critical for you to provide the type of support that will have a real impact on your work together. Explain your value and what's in it for the executive. Another option would be to get clear on how this executive prefers to communicate. Ask the question, "What is the best way to communicate with you to get responses that will enable me to execute on the tasks I need to perform on your behalf?" You may also have to get creative. As an example, weekly roundup emails, as I like to call them, is one way to do that. Each week, keep a running list of all the items you need your executives input on and compile and send in one email at the end or beginning of the week. Attach any corresponding information like previous emails that give context to what is on your list. This is one of my favorite ways to get what I need from a busy executive. It gives them a concise list with attachments to reference, and they can provide a response without taking the time to get on a phone or video call. It's also important that when you can get time for a phone or video call, that you tailor your communication in a way that leads to a productive exchange for you and the executive. In this case, this executive did not want all the details of everything the assistant was working on. Instead, to effectively communicate would require the assistant to finesse their conversations with hard facts and solutions on how she could help her. When she began to show up at one-on-ones with an intentional list of smart questions as well as recommendations for improved administrative productivity, over time, she was able to convince her executive that she could be trusted and would add value. This approach drastically improved how they communicated and led to a more beneficial partnership.

As a bonus, building a relationship with your PBD can frequently open doors to potential opportunities. When you have advocates who understand your aspirations for career advancement, they often utilize their influence and connections to assist you in progressing toward your desired professional destination. The power of tapping into other's networks and platforms is essential to the next Marketing strategy: Build Relationships.

EVOLUTIONARY EXERCISE

After you've identified your PBD, schedule a time to meet with each of them. The following are some examples of questions to ask your board.

- What do you consider to be my key strengths and areas of expertise?

- In your opinion, what are the areas where I have shown the most growth and improvement?

- Are there any specific skills or knowledge areas that you think I should focus on developing further?

- How would you describe my communication style and effectiveness? Are there any areas where I could enhance my communication skills?

- Can you provide feedback on my ability to work in teams or collaborate with others?

- What do you think sets me apart from others in my field or role?

- Are there any blind spots or areas where I may be overlooking opportunities for improvement?

- How would you describe my level of initiative and proactivity in taking on new challenges or projects?

- Do you have any suggestions on how I can enhance my leadership abilities or take on more leadership roles?

- Are there any specific accomplishments or achievements of mine that you believe showcase my capabilities effectively?

Build Relationships

Take a minute and think about your typical day. What do you do in the morning when you first get to the in-person or virtual office? Who do you connect with throughout the day? Who are you meeting for lunch or turning to for insight and expertise?

If you're like many administrative professionals, you start your day and stay glued to your desk, steadfast, focusing on the tasks at hand. This is often what we've been trained to do and what we're hired for– to be there to efficiently support and address our team's needs. Yet to advance in your career, it's time to stop hiding behind your real or virtual desk and get visible.

Now that you have identified your personal brand and gained the insight of your Personal Board of Directors, to move to the next step in your evolution, make time to be in contact with others so they can see those strengths you're looking to highlight. Build a network of individuals that you might not typically interact with daily. Expand your horizons, get to know folks from all corners of the organization, and let them know who you are along with your unique contributions.

Some of this can be accomplished by simply dedicating time each day to connect with others at your organization. This could be through a brief catch-up conversation, an email congratulating a coworker on a job done well, or an offer to treat one of your colleagues to lunch. To deepen connections beyond your immediate circle, increase your network by participating in various groups and activities, such as employee resource groups, professional development opportunities, company-sponsored community service or employee wellness initiatives.

This type of engagement can help to build and fortify relationships with colleagues and enhance your overall organizational involvement. It also demonstrates your interest in, and commitment to, the company, which could be key when future opportunities arise outside your immediate circle of influence.

Other administrative professionals shared strategies they've used to build our networks.

"I have quick, 10-minute meeting every week with other administrative professionals during a time when the executives aren't in the office yet, because many of us get there way ahead of them. I tend to take that 10 minutes in the middle of the week to just hear what's going on in their area and with the individuals that they support. It's more of a support system and a way to check on them. Then sometimes we'll get drinks, because we spend so much time at work, we don't get to know individuals and what their needs are from the perspective of just their lives. Little things like that help retain people as well, and I think those are the little things that executives appreciate because they're not always thinking about it."

"When someone new comes on board, I like to reach out to them and say, 'Hey, welcome to the company. Let's grab a coffee.'"

"There's a huge benefit with not trying to get out of the office every day right at five. For me, I have executives that hang out until 6:30, and I've gained a lot of knowledge recently by being there after everyone's gone. The ruckus and the circus are over, and it's just you and your executive for 15, 20, or 30 minutes. You can pick their brain or have a discussion about the organization overall. I've gained a lot of interesting insights and been able to pick up on key things. it allows me to get some personal one-on-one time beyond the typical check-the-boxes 30-minute meeting. Instead, we have a casual, relaxing conversation, where I can really get what's on top of their mind and know their priorities."

Building relationships can put you in a position to learn more about potential career opportunities. Expanding your network and nurturing professional relationships makes you more visible to those around you and increases opportunities to showcase your growth. You never know when an opportunity might come knocking, and greatness isn't going to knock on an invisible door! Instead, when seeking to fill those opportunities, the decision-makers will often seek out those who have put in the work to be seen and heard.

A word of caution: Avoid narrowing your focus solely on building relationships with top-level leaders and neglecting others throughout the organization. You never know who may hold influence over your next opportunity or be in a position to choose your next career move. You also don't need to feel like you have to make connections with everyone who works for your organization. The reality is that some of your colleagues might be problematic employees, which can be true in any organization. Fortunately, relationship-building isn't a numbers game. It's less about just going out to meet a large number of people; it is to establish meaningful connections and align yourself with the right people. Connect with those that are successful in their ability to meet goals, regardless of their position. Build relationships with those who are generally well-liked, well received and on successful teams. Develop connections with individuals whom you can comfortably share insights and knowledge with, while also benefiting from their wisdom and experiences. Pay attention to all those components as you go out and build relationships. As you broaden your network, remember to choose your connections wisely, as relationships can significantly impact your reputation and influence the conversations happening about you, even in your absence.

In my previous organization, when a decision was made to build a new facility, I saw an opportunity. I realized that with the expansion, we would need a facilities manager for the new space. A little under a year before the new location was built, I took the initiative to develop a job description for the office management role and presented it to the executives I was supporting at the time, the President, and the CFO, making the case on why I would be the best fit. At the time, they could not say with certainty that the actual role would exist but absolutely appreciated my initiative and the time and detail I took to identify this potential position. In my mind, it also planted the seed with them that I was thinking about my career evolution and growth.

A few months before the actual move to the new building, the role of facilities manager became available, and I was encouraged to apply. Luckily, I had built a strong relationship with a colleague who was going to be involved in the hiring process for the new facilities department. Moreover, the reputation I built within the organization made the hiring team eager to meet with me. After several successful interviews with our executive team and the department manager, I secured the new position as facilities manager.

However, there was a catch. Although my executive supported my career aspirations, he asked if I would continue supporting him during the transition while they searched for my replacement. And while the new position seemed like the perfect opportunity that matched my career aspirations and came with a pay increase, I wasn't entirely thrilled about working for the new manager or facing the various challenges and issues that would come with the new position. I decided to seek advice from one of the members of my Personal Board of Directors, an executive within the company. I told him I was excited about the office management role, but there were significant problems within the new department. He wisely replied, "You are currently on a winning team, and you are choosing to move to a team with identified issues. While taking on new challenges is great, try to align yourself with winners as you navigate your career. Expanding your role on a winning team will take you even further."

What he was suggesting was that I consider staying in my existing role and exploring expansion, as opposed to moving into the new role. Empowered by this advice and leveraging my positive relationship with my executive, I went back to him and proposed an alternative. "I'm willing to stay and continue to provide you with administrative support, but only if we can find a way to expand my responsibilities and create a clear career path for me, allowing me to reach my financial goals." He fully supported the idea, and together we crafted a new management position that not only added exciting responsibilities but also helped me achieve my financial objectives. This opportunity allowed me to step into a leadership role within the organization on a team poised for success.

This personal journey to success is a real-life example of how building a strong network and aligning yourself with winners can lead to remarkable career rewards. It may take time and require you to step out of your comfort zone, but the results are worth it. Remember, you deserve to be seen, heard, and recognized in your career.

Carve Your Career Path

I'm going to start this section with a truth that you probably already know by now: **You cannot wait around for your organization to hand you a career plan on a silver platter.** You've got to take the reins and build that plan yourself. You are the architect of your own career. Explore other roles. Once you find one that you are interested in, take time to understand what skills are needed for the role and work to fill in any gaps to ensure that your skill set aligns with your ambitions. Then, when those opportunities knock, you'll be ready to swing that door wide open.

A career path is a roadmap for our personal and professional development. As I navigated my career journey, I recognized the importance of charting a deliberate path that aligned with my aspirations and growth objectives. This led me to pursue the role of facilities manager, a strategic move aimed at propelling my professional development forward. The facilities manager position was a step up from my previous one, and in the new department there was a clear upward progression.

To position myself for the role, I identified both my skills and areas for improvement. For example, my tenure of over five years with the company and time working in the President's Office provided valuable experience and gave me insights into what would benefit the employee base. However, I also recognized gaps in my knowledge and lack of formal facilities management training. To address these gaps, I dedicated time to researching facilities management as a discipline. This helped me gain clarity on the role's requirements and identify opportunities for additional training to enhance my skill set. And while I ultimately made the decision to remain in my support role with the commitment from my manager to expand it, without a deliberate approach to pursuing advancement, this newly imagined role may not have ever become a reality.

One powerful strategy to advance to a higher role within the administrative field is to get to know the administrative professional who sits in the seat you dream of occupying. For instance, if you currently support a director but aspire to support a vice president or even the CEO, consider learning about the skills that helped the person in that role succeed and gain a comprehensive understanding of the job from their perspective. If there's an opportunity to establish a rapport and build a relationship with that individual within your organization, I would encourage you to do so. Learn more about the role through their lens. If you can't do it at your own company, connect with someone in a similar role at a different company. State your intention by communicating that they would be someone you could learn from as you create your career path.

In the introduction, I mentioned that my experience at a large Midwest company proved pivotal to my understanding of the possibilities of an administrative role. My perception of the assistants supporting senior management underwent a significant transformation as I observed how they were viewed and treated within the organization. They functioned as integral members of their executives' teams and were viewed as more than support staff; they were actively involved in high-level meetings and were encouraged by leadership to expand their knowledge beyond their job descriptions. Their expertise in process improvements and business matters gave them influence in decision-making. Actively seeking professional growth, they attended seminars and workshops and earned certifications. They played a key role in company events and organizational activities and fostered collaboration and community among administrative professionals through networking and knowledge-sharing. Their presence set the standard for excellence; inspiring others like me. I vividly recall one assistant who took me under her wing, offering valuable insights into the role at that level.

You may have a general idea of what someone's job entails but being up close to them lets you gain a real and specific understanding of their work. This point of view can provide you with clarity on what it will take for you to get from where you are to where you would like to be.

This can be incredibly helpful even if you aspire to a role outside of the administrative professional space. I once worked with an assistant who had a passion for writing and aspired to transition from the assistant role into the field of communications. I advised her to seek knowledge from employees in the communications department. You might also seek opportunities to learn from professionals in the desired field outside your organization to gain a deeper understanding of their work. Engage in insightful conversations to gather, understand, and determine the key requirements for success.

You've got to be an active participant in carving out your career even when you can't see the direct connections to help you get there. You may not have everything required to get to the next level yet but help from others will allow you to be better prepared when opportunities arise. I tell the assistants on my team to act like they sit in the next seat, because if that person's next opportunity comes along, that seat's going to be empty. Be ready to fill it!

Challenging Office Culture

If you're reading this and, instead of feeling empowered by this framework, you're feeling frustrated, don't give up! That frustration may very well come from the challenge of trying to implement these steps in a difficult work environment that is not supportive of your growth.

Remember **your focus should be on *you* and not the environment around you.** Admittedly there are some workplaces where this journey to evolve is much harder than others. Personal evolution isn't easy to accomplish no matter where you work, but the process is much smoother when you have a team rallying around you rather than one where you feel like you're being met with opposition blocking your progress at every turn. I wish I had a shortcut to offer you, but there really is no way around it. Creating change for yourself in an unhealthy office environment is more challenging and is going to require you to develop the mental fortitude and ability to power through the difficulties and do what's best for you. And while the process is harder, it's not impossible.

To evolve when your workplace is challenging, keep the following principles in mind.

- Lean into your Personal Board of Directors. When the going gets tough, you need a squad of trusted confidantes who've got your back. Remember, these are the people who lift you up, give you that reality check, and provide the support and guidance you need. They're your secret weapon and can be a source of wisdom in the midst of chaos. Leverage those individuals for what information and resources they may have and lean on them for extra support and motivation when you need it. Please note your PBD is not just an outlet for you to complain. Be sure to genuinely value and heed some of their advice and try to balance your attitude when speaking with them so you don't run the risk of burning them out.

- Sharpen your skills. Don't let the challenges within your current environment prevent you from up-skilling to get to where you need to be. You may not be able to find a new job immediately, and you may not be able to change the work environment, but you can change yourself with continuous learning and improvement. What you cannot do is allow an environment to limit progress. Doing that is a hard No. Whether a new opportunity eventually arises in your organization, or you ultimately decide you need to start looking elsewhere, a solid skillset will be critical to your advancement.

- Operate with excellence in all that you do. There are a lot of employees who spend time complaining about the organizations in which they work, without taking inventory of themselves and determining where their own work needs improvement. Before you conclude that your job is limiting you and your organization is holding you back, make sure that the way you're performing right now is with a high degree of excellence. If you are not doing so, you can't expect your manager or organization to be committed to your development. Even if you decide your best option is to change jobs, remember that you're going to take yourself with you to the next office, so if you don't rule yourself out as the problem now, you may find yourself in the same situation at the next workplace.

- Guard Your Emotions. A challenging office culture can undoubtedly take a toll on your emotional well-being. Recognize and acknowledge your emotions when faced with difficult people or situations. Bottling up your feelings is rarely a healthy option, as it can lead to increased stress and frustration, lower mental and physical energy, and impair productivity as your negative emotions fester within you. In such moments, remind yourself that feelings are not always a reflection of reality. They are subjective responses to circumstances and can be influenced by various factors. Simply put, feelings are not facts.

- Maintain a journal. It's a safe space to express your feelings, reflect on them, and gain perspective over time.

I understand that working through these principles in a challenging work environment can be extraordinarily difficult, especially if you get resistance from others at your organization or even from your manager. But this book is all about your personal evolution and transformation; it is about committing to yourself. It's easy to let frustration get the best of you, but while you may not have the power to shift the entire office culture, you have complete control over your own mindset and actions. **Your environment may be tough, but I believe you are tougher.** Embrace that power, rise above negativity, and get ready for the better opportunity coming your way.

CHAPTER SUMMARY

- Your personal brand is about how others see you. Being an administrative professional puts us in the position to be able to leverage our close proximity to the decision-makers at our organizations. Develop a personal brand statement to tap into your authentic strengths and help guide your activities.

- Your Personal Board of Directors is comprised of your evolution champions. Select three or four people who are affected by your work to provide you with feedback as part of your Board. Be open to their feedback and use it to highlight your strengths and fill in any professional gaps.

- To engage in relationship building, market yourself by getting visible at your job. Be intentional in connecting with colleagues through informal activities and company events and align yourself with winners as you navigate your career path.

- Your organization is not going to chart your career for you; it's up to you to carve out your career path. Get to know the person in the role you want so that you can learn what you need to do to get there and prepare yourself with the skills you need to occupy that dream role so that you'll be ready when it becomes available.

- Creating change in a challenging office environment requires resilience. Lean on your Personal Board of Directors to get through the difficulties, focus on your professional development until you get a new opportunity, and make sure you're operating with excellence in your job performance.

Maintenance

A TALE OF TWO ASSISTANTS

Amanda, unfortunately, found herself struggling to reach the Maintenance phase. After all, how could she maintain something that she never prioritized in the first place? She had not yet shifted her mindset towards adopting and sustaining the behaviors necessary for success. While she possessed the skills required for her position, Amanda lacked the determination to actively improve and refine her abilities. Consequently, she found it challenging to maintain a consistent practice of behaviors that she had not fully embraced.

Tanya, in contrast, had transformed into a more deliberate and tactical assistant. Recognizing the significance of understanding her organization's priorities and the industry as a whole, Tanya decided to educate herself further. This newfound knowledge empowered her to confidently manage meetings on the calendar, understanding their purpose and strategic placement. Tanya even had the confidence to speak on behalf of her manager when interacting with stakeholders and, on occasion, act as a proxy for her manager in important meetings.

Through continuous evolution, Tanya realized she needed to enhance her PowerPoint skills. With the support of her manager, she decided to take a course and diligently practiced in order to improve. As a testament to her growth, her work in PowerPoint was utilized in a presentation to the CEO, showcasing the value she brought to the organization. With a deeper understanding of her workplace, Tanya even offered a valuable suggestion for creating a new onboarding process, ensuring a consistent, elevated experience for new employees entering the company.

Tanya also continued to expand her network by leaning into the wisdom of her Personal Board of Directors and finding ways to connect with colleagues in other areas of her organization. These efforts benefited Tanya through new connections and insights and served as a platform for others to witness her talents, even those who may not regularly interact with her in her day-to-day work.

As she consistently implemented the Mindset, Management, and Marketing principles, Tanya found the sweet spot that so many aspire to in their work. The pieces began to fit together, and the principles started to flow. While she remained ever mindful of the process, embodying each principle began to feel natural, and incorporating the qualities of an Evolved Assistant fit seamlessly into her everyday work.

Tanya knew that the process was ongoing and that there was always room for growth, but when she looked at the path she had traveled and how far she had come from feeling frustrated, stuck, and stagnant in her career, Tanya knew one thing for sure. She had evolved.

If you've ever taken part in any type of transformational program, you know that once you reach the maintenance phase, it's time to celebrate. The effort you undertook to transition from your initial state to the transformed one you're in now has been accomplished. You can look back at where you were when you started your journey and see the results of your work.

Take a moment to reflect on your path to where you are currently. Have you recognized any small wins? Has your outlook on what is possible expanded? Are there aspects of managing your workflow that have become easier for you? Whether your growth has been substantial, or you've progressed only a few steps, take a moment to celebrate your development and reward yourself with a well-deserved acknowledgement.

Now, it can be tempting at this phase to say, "I have arrived," give yourself a high-five and move on. But while getting to the maintenance phase takes work, staying there also takes effort.

Have you ever heard about the maintenance phase of weight loss being the most challenging? Individuals shed weight using various approaches and often feel elated as they observe the number on the scale diminish, leading them closer to their target weight. However, a stark fact remains. Approximately 90% of those who undergo substantial weight loss eventually regain it, often exceeding their original weight.

People get so focused on weight loss because that's the exciting part. That's where they achieve the most progress and see the most visible wins. They work whatever program will get them across the finish line, but many methods don't include a solid strategy for what happens when they get there.

The key to any successful transformation is being able to sustain the progress that you've made. This is why maintenance is included as a part of this framework. Maintenance isn't just about getting to a point and staying where you are; it's about fine-tuning your Mindset, Management, and Marketing to continue to build on your current success, grow, and live out the concepts you've adopted and implemented. Remember, the need for continued growth doesn't disappear even if you've reached a place where you are content and aren't looking to advance to a new career position, because your organization and the expectations of the role will continue to grow and change. By now, I hope I've stressed the point enough that continued evolution is essential no matter where we are in our career journey. We may be happy where we are, but we still run the risk of being left behind if we get to one place and stand still.

As you observe the tangible results you're achieving, it becomes a time to celebrate your accomplishments. Additionally, you have the opportunity to assess and refine other areas that require further growth, ensuring your progression along the path of becoming an Evolved Assistant.

In this phase, you'll reap the benefits of your growth. You'll work confidently in your expanded role, with the knowledge that you are an indispensable asset to your organization. Your colleagues and coworkers will see you as an essential contributor to the team's success, and they'll feel the impact of your expertise.

In my own experience, invitations were strong indicators of this.

- Invitations into conversations that were about making decisions on employee impacting changes within the office

- Invitations to help hire, coach, and train assistants that were not my direct reports

- Invitations to speak to teams within my organization about my career journey and how my work directly influences that of the leaders of our organization

Gone are the days of feeling invisible and unheard. Maintenance is where people continue to regularly see you, recognize your worth, and appreciate what you bring to the table. You will have solidified your standing as a force of influence within your organization, and as a bonus, you might have the power to drive change and reshape how others perceive the work of administrative professionals overall. Simply by standing in your excellence, you'll start to break down those outdated stereotypes!

This is your opportunity to capitalize on your visibility, unleash your full potential, and revel in your progress while you continuously refine your skills and expertise.

Let's jump in and explore how to maintain your progress on this evolution journey.

Discretionary Effort

One of the exciting things about maintenance is that you've gotten into a rhythm. You're implementing the other three principles and starting to gain your stride. Now that you have mastered the essential areas, it's time to kick it up a notch with discretionary effort to take your work beyond the realm of requirements. You've already mastered the basics; now it's time for a little razzle-dazzle.

Discretionary effort is the magic touch that sets you apart. It's when you give that extra little sprinkle of icing on the cake and provide unexpected gestures that leave a lasting impression. Discretionary effort includes those sparks that transform your ordinary tasks into extraordinary ones.

Here's the important piece to remember about discretionary efforts; they're called "discretionary" for a reason. It's up to you to decide when and where you put in these efforts. According to Oxford Languages, discretion is "the freedom to decide what should be done in a particular situation." This is not about feeling like you need to break your back to reach for the stars whenever someone asks you to perform a task. Instead, it is about determining where you would like to make those extra efforts based on your own assessment of what you can manage and where you feel they will make an impact.

Think about it like when you go to a restaurant where the servers bring you a slice of chocolate cake that you didn't order. It is the extra small gestures you may not have been expecting but getting them contributes to your satisfaction with the experience. Use your discretion to decide when to offer "treats" to those in your organization and identify places where making time to take an extra small step will provide a big impact.

"I try to anticipate what my leaders need," shared an administrative professional. "When they go on a trip, for example, I put all the information that's on the itinerary on one page, including an abbreviated agenda, getting from point A to point B and every step along the way. I include a little note about what the weather is supposed to be, and the dress code for the meetings. Anything I can think of that might be helpful for them. I often include maps and directions if they have a multi-facility visit, especially if they're renting a car. I keep a file on each of my leaders and I include things like their staff's birthdays, then put those on the calendar so that they know when it's a special day for one of their team members. One of my leaders asks me to keep all her passwords for all of her associations and every professional group that she belongs to. When she goes to a website, she'll call me for her username and ID, and I'll have that information for her in a flash. Little things like that sometimes just let them know that they can call on me and I can give them what they need in a moment."

This type of effort does not always have to be a physical task; it can also take the form of a recommendation or suggestion. Over the span of my career, I have supported executives that have hectic and busy schedules. I've noticed that many of them habitually say yes to everything, without considering if these engagements are the best use of their time or if they are moving the needle forward in their business. I believe that as assistants, we can give those we support permission to do something different. I know that may sound like an odd way to say it, but I think we gain a perspective about their work that they will sometimes miss because of the pace at which they are operating. For instance, we can ask, "You had dinner with that client two weeks ago. Do you need to meet again, or can you send someone on your behalf?" Or suggest, "You haven't met with this person during your weekly slot for the last three weeks. I recommend adjusting the meeting cadence to ensure you are able to meet and it's productive time well spent." While it may feel uncomfortable at first to guide them differently, I've seen it provoke valuable reflection on how they spend their time and real appreciation for receiving the guidance.

Discretionary effort goes a long way in that people notice the special touches, the contributions we make that enhance the work environment of those we support. Your colleagues remember when you have gone above and beyond to create an experience that exceeds their expectations. In addition, there is self-satisfaction when that discretionary effort is acknowledged. It contributes to the joy, personal satisfaction, and fulfillment in your work.

Become Indispensable

In this maintenance phase, something truly magical happens. You start feeling the tangible impact of your contributions. Your value becomes evident, not only to yourself but to others as well. Executives, team members, and others in your organization respect what you do and see you as a key player in their success. You're not just a support function anymore; you're a vital force within the organization adding value daily.

You may notice that people begin to call on you and reach out to you as a subject matter expert on various topics. Now that you are managing tasks with excellence and efficiency and marketing yourself so that others know your skill set, they'll seek your input in the areas where you shine. Your insights and expertise will be in demand as others recognize the depth of your knowledge and understanding of the business, its processes, and people.

You may find yourself stepping into new areas and participating in events and activities that you hadn't been involved in before. You may increasingly be invited to the table of influence and decision-making. Your voice matters, and people want to hear it.

Sure, we all know that no one is truly irreplaceable in the workplace. But it is important to believe that you bring certain qualities to your work that are indispensable and unique to you. There's a confidence you will start to feel when you understand that what you do and how you do it truly makes a difference. You understand that you hold the power to shape the work environment, enhance the experiences of those around you, and bring a sense of purpose to your interactions. Knowing that you have the power to spark positive change and leave a lasting imprint is vital to your continued maintenance and growth.

This feeling and knowledge about being indispensable comes about in different ways for different individuals for a variety of reasons. "I would say that mine is simply because I have been in the same role for so many years," shared one assistant. "Mine is sheer knowledge of that company. Of course, I can do the job, but a lot of it is the knowledge that I've garnered for all these years. I don't think anybody can't be let go or changed or anything at any time. But I do feel just the fact that I've had so much longevity at my company gives me an advantage."

"I think for me, the skill is influence," shared another. What I mean by that is not influence because of my title, I think you can have influence with any title if it's relational influence. I saw it play out in my EA role. I was able to influence the entire culture of the administrative discipline at this organization. And now in my new role, and when I think about the skill of influence, I think about being the person who others say, 'we can't even make that decision without including this person and what they have to say about this.' That doesn't come from the title. It comes from the relationships that you build and being an expert in your field."

Working with executives over the years, one of the qualities that I feel has made me indispensable is the ability to combine my knowledge, skills, and experience of the business and its people to help executives make decisions. It is always my goal to develop the type of relationship with any executive I support where there is mutual trust and respect. I am invested in their success, so I take time to understand who they are personally and professionally, their priorities, and what makes them able to show up and focus their energy and efforts on what matters to the business.

Let me explain.

Being the boss can be a lonely position. For many of the people we support, particularly those in upper management, it can be tough for them to have people around whom they trust and with whom they can discuss confidential matters. The responsibility of making employee-impacting decisions that you cannot discuss with anyone is a tough spot, especially if it impacts their employment. One such example was when an executive that I supported needed to make some changes in her organization. Some of her direct reports were not performing well or meeting their goals, and others were not in roles that aligned with their skill sets. She had to make some tough decisions and needed to be thoughtful about whether to move people to other roles or remove them from the organization.

That's where I came in.

She needed to talk through these changes. What she didn't realize is that I had observed what was happening within the organization and formulated my own thoughts about who should move to other roles and who should probably be removed from the team. She called me in her office and, with her organizational chart printed, began to talk through each person, their skill set, their contributions, and whether they worked well with the team. I was able to serve as a sounding board for her and also provide valuable contributions to the discussion based on my own observations and insight. For her, I could sense a bit of relief to be able to discuss this with someone that she trusted and make decisions about this confidently. The people we support feel it when we are invested in them. All of us want to be supported in our work and executives, leaders, and managers are no different.

It takes time to get to the place of feeling indispensable, but when you do, embrace this newfound sense of indispensability with open arms. Embrace the knowledge that your work matters, that your presence is valued, and that you are making a profound difference. Let it fuel your passion, your commitment, and your dedication to continue walking along the Evolved Assistant path.

Experience Flow

Picture this: you've entered a realm where your groove is your sanctuary. You're in complete harmony with your work, and your thoughts align with your purpose. The days of self-doubt, negative thoughts, and pointing fingers are behind you. You have gained clarity and shifted your mindset. You understand what you can control and what is beyond your influence. You've claimed ownership of your journey, and it's empowering.

You're not just thinking about your tasks. You're implementing the other three principles of the framework. You're managing, learning, and building relationships with determination. You seek feedback, engage with the community at work, and actively grow in your role. These actions pave the way for the flow that makes your work feel like a natural extension of yourself. The discomfort and disruptions begin to fade away.

"I think I'm probably in a flow best when I am under pressure," an administrative professional said. "And when I am more stressed, or things are tougher, I seem to get in a much better flow. I help plan and attend a lot of big meetings. And when we have almost 3000 of us at an out-of-town conference and there are so many working parts, something just seems to click, and I get in the flow. Just a few weeks ago, 16 of us had an off-site meeting out of state. I planned it all, and there was a lot of pressure to make sure everything went okay. But those are the times when I feel like I'm really, really in my groove–when I think there's a lot more pressure on me. So, while it's stressful, I do feel like that's when I really can step up and perform and feel really like it's, it's going. It's working."

As you progress through the maintenance phase, you'll experience the very essence of what you set out to achieve. The evolution may be slow and gradual, but every step forward brings you closer to finding your place and understanding your true value. You're no longer just a cog in the machine; you're a vital piece of the puzzle that drives success.

Those who haven't shifted will find it difficult to embrace this flow. They'll feel unsettled, constantly searching for something they can't quite grasp. It's in the pursuit of growth and transformation that the magic truly unfolds.

One administrative professional shared the magic she experienced from organizing an international conference. "We held a team summit outside of the United States and it was sort of like my show. It was a full week, and we were flying people in from all over the world. The two months leading up to that and the stresses the planning involved were so great, but one thing I did that I highly recommend for any sort of big event or presentation was to do a step-by-step playbook. I included everything down to when my boss walked into the conference room that first day, I had the music playing, I had the people sitting, I had everything going, and it just went seamlessly. I lived by that playbook the whole week. And one of our international executives actually came up to me towards the end, and said, 'I've been to conferences all over the world, but this one just was the top.' It just felt really good. It was very successful."

As someone who has done the work, I want you to lean into this feeling of flow. There will be obstacles and setbacks along the way, but always keep in mind that this journey requires endurance and persistence. Focus on progress and not perfection. Take on the challenges, learn from them, and let them propel you forward.

CHAPTER SUMMARY

- The maintenance phase is about sustaining and building upon your progress. It's not just about reaching a goal, but continuing to grow and adapt as your role and organization evolve.

- Discretionary effort sets you apart. It's about going beyond basic requirements and adding extra value to your work, using your judgment to decide when and where to apply these efforts.

- Becoming indispensable means your colleagues and executives recognize your unique value. You're seen as a key player whose insights and expertise are sought after.

- Experience flow when you're in harmony with your work. This comes from consistently applying the principles of Mindset, Management, and Marketing, leading to a natural rhythm in your role. Embrace the feeling of making a difference. Understand that your work matters and your presence is valued, which fuels your passion and commitment to continue evolving.

Beyond Maintenance

A TALE OF TWO ASSISTANTS

One year later...

As offices slowly began to re-open, Amanda found herself facing an uncertain future. Her organization was making decisions about bringing employees back to the office, and Amanda's department had been deemed permanently virtual. While she had initially felt frustrated and stagnant in the virtual work environment, she had come to accept it as her new normal and decided to continue working from home.

However, just a few weeks after the decision was made, Amanda received a call from her boss that shattered her sense of security. They informed her that her role was no longer needed. Due to the virtual nature of her department, they felt that the work Amanda had been doing could be easily divided between two other administrative assistants. They offered her a position that had reduced responsibilities in another department, accompanied by a pay cut. Amanda was devastated and felt a mix of anger, hurt, and frustration. She had been a loyal employee and believed her dedication should have been rewarded, not met with demotion, and decreased pay.

Feeling stuck and uncertain about her next steps, Amanda decided to attend a workshop she discovered through a resource group for administrative assistants. It focused on taking charge of one's career, and it was there that she found inspiration in the success story of Tanya, an administrative assistant who had thrived despite challenges.

Tanya's journey hadn't been perfect; she had faced her fair share of stress and frustration. However, she had managed to find her groove and navigate the daily obstacles with resilience. Her commitment to personal growth had paid off, and she had become an expert in her field, particularly excelling in creating outstanding presentations.

Meanwhile, the company had begun making plans for a hybrid work model, with employees returning to the office. As a result, a new office manager position became available, and Tanya was privy to this opportunity through her strong connections within the organization. Her skills and talents had garnered glowing reviews, leading some of the company's leaders to encourage her to apply for the role.

In the past, Tanya would have been intimidated by the increased responsibilities of the office manager position. However, her personal growth had prepared her for this very moment. She had diligently worked on expanding her skill set and was ready to embrace the new challenge. Tanya underwent a series of interviews with the department, impressing them with her expertise, and ultimately, she secured the role. Not only did it come with more responsibility, but also a well-deserved raise.

Although Tanya's journey had its share of challenges, she was genuinely content with the strides she had made. Being an Evolved Assistant was no longer just a means to an end; it had become a way of life that she was committed to maintaining for her future.

Inspired by Tanya's story, Amanda began to believe that she, too, could carve out a brighter future by embracing change and investing in her own personal and professional growth.

Congratulations!

You've made it through the framework. You've got your **Mindset** together. You're **Managing** projects like a pro and **Marketing** your skills so everyone can see how brightly your work shines. Most importantly, you're **Maintaining** your progress and tweaking, testing, and refining each step so that your path is one of continuous improvement.

You are an Evolved Assistant. And no matter where you are in your evolution, be proud of yourself for getting to this point and becoming a part of this community.

Now that you're here, let me tell you something that, if you've truly been doing the work to becoming an Evolved Assistant, you likely already know:

This work doesn't stop at Maintenance. The pandemic was a wake-up call, reminding us that life can surprise us with unexpected challenges that prompt us to reevaluate our positions and contemplate the unknown future. However, a global pandemic is not the only thing that can throw us off course and alter our direction. Change is a constant presence, both in our personal lives and professional journeys. Instead of evading change or instinctively deeming it negative, view each change as a chance to assess your personal evolution and progress. It's an opportunity to revisit what you've learned and consider how you can apply those lessons to adapt and continue progressing.

The 4Ms Framework is our survival kit, our guideline on this journey to becoming Evolved Assistants. But this journey won't be a straight shot. You will encounter some triggers and obstacles: A shift in your organization, a change in leadership, or even a new job opportunity. A new role might require you to market yourself in a different way. Changing responsibilities may alter the way you need to manage your projects. Working with a new manager could mean a shift in mindset, or a change in your personal life could challenge the way you maintain it all. Fortunately, as an Evolved Assistant, you can now reassess your growth and re-visit the 4Ms with the confidence of knowing that you will once again arrive at the place you want to be.

In my own work, I've experienced this at different organizations with changes in leadership. New leaders bring a new outlook and often different expectations for administrative professionals. Suddenly, we're asked to show up in ways that we've never had to before. These aren't once-in-a-lifetime events like a global pandemic. These changes happen in organizations every day and are prime examples of how external circumstances can impact our roles, making it critical to continue to implement the principles we've established.

Transitioning to support a new executive marked a significant change in my professional journey. This shift brought unexpected challenges as I navigated unfamiliar territory with this executive. From my perspective, she seemed unaccustomed to having a support leader, like me, who had become a true partner to my executive and considered an asset to the business. This lack of understanding led to a disconnect in our working relationship, where I felt undervalued and overlooked.

Her expectations for my role diminished my previous level of responsibility and influence. Managing her calendar and travel arrangements were table stakes for me, tasks I could perform without much effort. What I struggled with the most was my reduced involvement in planning large meetings or contributing to office decisions that impacted employees. I had been relegated to the responsibilities of a more junior assistant, significantly reducing the scope of my work. This shift left me feeling stagnant in my career growth and development. I was dissatisfied and frustrated.

To navigate this challenging dynamic, I turned to the 4Ms Framework.

Mindset: I acknowledged my initial discomfort but refused to let it overshadow my attitude. Recognizing that all new relationships undergo a period of adjustment, I maintained confidence in my abilities and remained optimistic that things would improve over time. Additionally, I leaned on my resilience and determination to persevere through the uncertainty.

Management: I proactively showcased my expertise and commitment to delivering high-quality work. By consistently demonstrating my capabilities, I aimed to establish myself as a valuable asset to the executive and the organization as a whole.

Marketing: I sought to build a rapport with the executive, emphasizing my skills and professional interests to foster a mutually beneficial partnership. Through open communication and collaboration, I aimed to position myself as a trusted ally in achieving our shared goals.

Maintenance: I focused on strategies for maintaining and nurturing the relationship over time. Such as regular check-ins, seeking feedback, and adjusting as necessary to ensure a positive and productive working relationship.

Despite my efforts to adapt and overcome the challenges, the dynamic with this executive ultimately served as a catalyst for me to explore new professional opportunities. Recognizing the importance of aligning myself with supportive and collaborative leaders, I made the decision to pursue a path that better aligned with my career aspirations and values. It proved to be the best decision.

In this Beyond Maintenance section, Let's examine ways that you can continue to grow long after you've gone through the Evolved Assistant framework.

Intentionality

Intentionality is the practice of making deliberate and conscious decisions, actions, or choices based on a clear purpose or goal. We adopted the mindset of taking charge of our own career way back in the first principle. But this intentionality around what we want for ourselves is the first thing to slide once we get comfortable. This slip is, in a way, the paradox of professional growth. After you get that coveted role you've been looking for, and the one that your evolution allowed you to grasp, it's easy to feel like you can coast, which can be a catalyst for you to backslide into old behaviors.

Inevitably, this desire to just sail along in our careers can put us right back into playing the waiting game down the line. After the newness of the current position fades, we're right back to waiting for someone to promote us, for someone to invest in our development, and for that moment when our dreams magically come true.

You have to take a continuous intentional approach to your career to grab the reins and steer your professional journey in the direction you desire. We all do.

Now, this doesn't necessarily mean that you're constantly racing up the career ladder or that you can never be happy and content where you are. Whether you're actively searching for your next role, or you wish to remain in your current position until retirement, what's important is to take time to reexamine and gain absolute clarity about your goals, regardless of where you currently stand. This way, you won't be caught off guard when the next inevitable change emerges.

And then you'll want to intentionally check in with yourself. Just like many organizations do periodic evaluations of their employees, make it a point to regularly check in with yourself and make sure your mindset, branding, and skills are still relevant and up to date. Evaluate whether you have the same career outlook and whether you're on track to meeting your career goals. Grab an ink pen and pull out that journal and ask what do I want to achieve? Where do I see myself in the future? Do my activities align with where I want to go?

Yes, you already asked yourself these questions. Yet, the fact that you responded a certain way six months ago doesn't guarantee those answers still hold true today. And let's face it, they'll probably shift in one, five, or ten years from now. It's essential to have a clear end goal in sight, whether it's advancing to new horizons or cultivating deep roots where you currently are. Without a destination in mind, you'll end up wandering aimlessly once more, feeling lost and dependent on someone else's guidance.

I make it a deliberate practice to check in with myself quarterly. I set a reminder on my calendar to do so. Sometimes we get so consumed with work and our personal lives that we do not take the time to be still and introspective. Reflecting on my career and personal well-being is a habit I've cultivated over time, and it was inspired by the wisdom of an executive I once worked with. During performance reviews, she emphasized her concern for my happiness, health, and overall fulfillment. Her genuine desire was to ensure that I found my work fulfilling, rewarding, and aligned with my personal growth and values. She wanted me to feel a sense of accomplishment and understand how my contributions positively impacted not only my own journey but also the success of the entire team.

I have taken that same approach with myself over the years, and when I have those moments of internal quiet, I always start with the question, "Self, are you happy, healthy, and whole?" I encourage you to adopt a similar practice in your own life. Regularly take a step back, be still, and honestly evaluate your well-being and satisfaction to help you gain valuable insights into how to shape a more fulfilling and rewarding career path for yourself.

Once you've reassessed your goals, action follows. Remember, as an Evolved Assistant, we don't wait for opportunities. We create them ourselves. Once we identify our goals, we seek out projects that align with them and identify where we need to level up to complete those tasks with excellence. Keep in mind the idea that you do not need to rely on others to invest in your professional development. Tasks, technology, and projects will continue to change, and it is always up to you to take charge and find those learning opportunities to help you grow. Attend workshops, pursue additional certifications, or even hire a mentor to guide you. You are the CEO of your career, so be sure to invest in yourself with the development that you deserve.

Staying intentional may also require you to revisit the Marketing principle. As you progress in your professional journey, how you wish to be perceived and the reputation you aspire to establish within your organization might undergo changes. Being intentional extends beyond sheer dedication and tireless effort. Find ways to showcase your expertise and know when it's time to master and highlight a different skill in your toolbox.

Intentionality keeps you grounded on the Evolved Assistant path. Keeping what you want, where you're going, and how you plan to get there top of mind helps you sidestep the temptation to coast along, waiting for someone to hand you success on a platter. Grab it with both hands and make it your own so that you can continue charting your path forward, one intentional step at a time.

Negativity

Throughout this book, I've talked a lot about the importance of confidence and how everything from outdated perceptions to hierarchy to gaps in skill and professional development can lead many administrative professionals to lack the confidence they need to attain success. If you are an administrative professional who lacked confidence prior to embarking on your Evolved Assistant journey, I hope that you have gained the boost you need as you've worked through the framework.

Adopting the right mindset and recognizing your administrative expertise boosts your confidence by affirming the value and significance of your work. Leveling up your Management and tapping into your skills and abilities transforms you from feeling voiceless to being unafraid to speak up in meetings or advocate for yourself in situations where it is needed.

Embracing the Marketing principle creates in you a willingness to shine in a situation where you may have previously been tempted to hide.

This space of confidently moving in the direction of your goals is where you want to be, but as you're riding along in your confident flow, be aware of a pothole that could threaten to derail your progress: negativity. To stay on the Evolved Assistant path, make it your mission to be vigilant in keeping negativity at bay.

If you spend much time on social media, you have probably seen stories and reels about the importance of keeping negative, toxic people away and not letting others bring you down. This is vitally important in both your professional and personal life. But before I get to those people, I want to deal with the person whose negativity can have the most profound impact on your progress: the inner critic. That person is you, or at least, that little voice inside your head that will, on occasion, spew negativity and self-doubt. When you're changing, growing, and evolving, that voice may try to tell you all sorts of things, and often it gets louder the more you grow. Imposter Syndrome, which you may have heard of, is a psychological phenomenon that can make you believe you don't deserve to be where you are, or you haven't earned your accomplishments. It may even try to convince you that you're incapable of learning or adapting to new things.

In *The Untethered Soul: The Journey Beyond Yourself*, author Michael Alan Singer states, "There is nothing more important to true growth than realizing that you are not the voice of the mind- you are the one who hears it."

Everyone deals with a negative inner voice at times, but the key is to know how to separate it from yourself and quiet it quickly. You are the receiver of the voice, but it is not "yours." Those negative whispers are nothing but fear and lies and are often not rooted in anything factual. You have earned every bit of your success, so whenever that inner voice starts spewing negativity, acknowledge it but then make the firm decision to move beyond it. Think, if the voice in your head were words coming out of an actual person's mouth, would you be friends with that person? I suspect not! Remind yourself of your worth, your capabilities, and the incredible growth you've achieved. Own your journey, and don't let negativity steal your shine.

The Untethered Soul includes several practical exercises and techniques described to help individuals move negative thoughts out of their minds.[6] It is one of my favorite books and has had a lasting impact on how I manage my own negative self-talk. One of the key exercises that Singer suggests is the practice of "not taking the bait" of negative thoughts.

The exercise involves recognizing that negative thoughts arise in the mind and consciously choosing not to engage with them or give them power. Singer suggests observing negative thoughts as if they are objects passing through your field of awareness, without attaching any emotional energy or identification to them.

By cultivating a sense of detachment and awareness, you can create distance between yourself and the negative thoughts, avoid getting caught up in the content of the thoughts or allowing them to influence your emotions, and prevent them from spiraling into rumination or affecting your overall well-being.

The two keys to this exercise are to consistently practice detachment and to observe our thoughts without judgment or involvement. Over time, this can lead to a greater sense of inner peace and freedom from the influence of negative thinking patterns. Conversely, when we fail to rein in negative thoughts, we sow seeds for limiting beliefs, which are unproductive thoughts or mindsets that we hold so firmly they feel like undeniable truths. Sadly, these beliefs can hold us back from doing things we want to do. And it's not just about how we see ourselves; they can also affect how we view the world, our ideas, and our interactions with people. We have acquired these deep-rooted beliefs through lessons from our parents and family, our personal life experiences, and even through our educational teachings, and they are present in all areas of our lives. While I consider myself a confident person, I can share that these beliefs have probably kept me from certain achievements throughout my life.

I've dealt with my own limiting beliefs.

- I am not a math person. I have never been good at math, and I never will be.

- I am an introvert, and I am not good at networking. I will not be able to build the relationships needed to grow my business.

- I am an assistant. No one would want to hear my point of view.

There are ways to overcome these, and the first is to acknowledge and identify your limiting beliefs. Be honest with yourself and then write them down. Next, you should determine whether any of these beliefs are coming from a place of accuracy. In my case, am I really not good at networking or is it just uncomfortable for me? When I am in a situation where I can network, do I walk away with a new contact or am I left without meeting someone new? The goal is to separate the facts from the stories you tell yourself. And finally, tell yourself positive affirmations to counteract those limiting beliefs. Reframe the negative self-talk, "I have the ability to build strong relationships through networking." Train your mind to see the positive in all situations.

Being able to tackle the negativity that comes from within is essential to staying on track, and learning to do this also sets a foundation for being able to conquer the negativity that may come from those around you. As you evolve and start showing up differently, confidently, and in spaces you haven't been in before, there may be naysayers questioning your presence in certain meetings or resisting your desire to be involved in detailed project discussions as examples. But when you've quieted your own negative voice, embraced your own value in your role, and identified exactly what you're trying to accomplish in your career, you can ward off their lack of understanding or acceptance as their problem, not yours.

There may be times when the best road to addressing negativity from someone else is to ignore it. In some instances, the best response to negativity is no response at all. Every negative engagement does not warrant a reaction from you. Your eyes are on a bigger prize so it's not worth it to expend your energy. In other instances, you may have to confront it head-on. If in fact you do need to confront someone directly, here are a few tips. First, maintain professionalism and avoid reacting emotionally. I would also not spend a great deal of time dwelling on any negativity. Remind yourself that their resistance does not define your worth or the value you bring to the workplace. Continue to confidently assert yourself, and don't allow others to let you doubt the importance of your role, the skills you possess, and the contributions you make.

Whether internal or external, it's important that you don't let negativity dim your shine or derail your success.

Recognize Your Genius

An image of Albert Einstein comes to mind for many when they hear the term "genius." Most associate it with someone who excels at academics or is a Master of Music or fine arts. Genius is not a term that is often used to describe our work as administrative professionals. But I believe it's time to change that.

We all have our own unique talents for supporting those we assist and enabling them to concentrate on their areas of expertise. We know how to step into problem-solve. We are skilled in analyzing situations, breaking them down into manageable parts, and providing clarity to those involved. We know how to create process and structure out of chaos. We can bring order and direction where others struggle. We are strategic thinkers, time savers, schedule managers, execution experts, organization gurus, process streamliners, systems creators, and solutions seekers. We are needs anticipators, information analysts, efficiency implementers, collaborators, relationship builders, culture influencers, and so much more.

Our powers are often overlooked, which is why it's critical that we recognize and celebrate the remarkable abilities we possess. By recognizing our own talents, we have the power to be changemakers. By owning our genius and standing in our roles with confidence and excellence, we can shift how our positions are perceived. There are so many aspects of our roles that go beyond performing administrative tasks and that set us apart. We can, and do, make meaningful impacts, shaping the culture of our teams and organizations in profound ways.

As you continue in your career as an Evolved Assistant, remember that staying cognizant of this and always advocating for your worth will both elevate your own career and help pave the road for other administrative professionals to evolve.

CHAPTER SUMMARY

- The journey of an Evolved Assistant doesn't end at Maintenance. Change is constant and each shift is an opportunity to reassess your growth and revisit the 4Ms Framework.

- Be intentional in your evolution. Make a practice to check in with yourself, reassess your goals, and align your actions with your aspirations to avoid becoming complacent.

- Remain vigilant in combatting negativity, both internal and external. Learn to quiet your inner critic and don't let others' negativity derail your progress.

- Recognize and celebrate your unique talents. Your skills represent a type of genius that can have meaningful impact in your organization.

- Continue to advocate for your worth and the value you bring to your organization. This not only elevates your own career but helps to create positive change for all administrative professionals.

Conclusion

When I first embarked on my journey to "get ready for the unknown," my primary goal was to make sure that I had job security in the face of a global pandemic. I could not have predicted that I would arrive at the place that would lead me to share my career lessons in this book. As I reflect on my career today, I find myself experiencing the sense of personal, professional, and financial fulfillment that I could only dream of as a new administrative professional nearly two decades ago. The path to self-discovery and empowerment that brought me from that space to where I stand today has not been without challenges, but it has been truly remarkable.

Becoming an Evolved Assistant is incredibly rewarding, yet we know the path to get there is not always easy. You will likely encounter moments that make you question the value of making this evolution and times when you feel like sliding back into old ways of operating. It's in the midst of those challenges that you will need to have the fortitude to keep pushing yourself forward. This fortitude—your own strength, courage, and determination in the face of adversity—is what will allow you to continue reaching for your goals when you feel like giving up. I have had times along the way when I felt like it might be easier to just coast along in my career, but I have learned to understand the power of my own strength to help carry me through those times. I believe that you have the capacity to do the same.

This journey hasn't just been about landing a fancy job title or securing a good salary. Those are of course great things to have, but it involves so much more. My path to becoming an Evolved Assistant has also been about recognizing the untapped potential within myself. This recognition has empowered me to take control of my career, shaping it in ways that enable me to construct the life I both desire and deserve. As a result:

I've discovered my voice—a voice that speaks not just of my accomplishments, but of the unique contributions I bring to the success of my executives and organizations. This voice has allowed me to champion the work we do and positioned me as an advocate for those who, like us, are dedicated to this profession.

Goals that once seemed distant are now within reach, and the satisfaction that comes from achieving them is immeasurable. I've found a solid footing in my career, standing strong in my understanding of my own potential and the possibilities that lie ahead.

I feel like a valued contributor in my role and an indispensable partner to the leaders I support and the team I manage. My own evolution has enabled me to serve as an impactful voice that matters to the culture, leadership, and success of my organization.

When I think back on my career and times of frustration, stagnation, and uncertainty, I realize that everything I needed to reach this place of fulfillment was already within me. It was a matter of recognizing my capabilities, accepting change, and embracing the Evolved Assistant framework.

And guess what? You're capable of the same shifts. It's okay if the future doesn't look completely clear. For me, my desire to become an expert voice recognized within the administrative professional community started with a single step. I did not know where the path would eventually lead, but I knew that by embracing the concepts that I have learned, and now shared with you, I would be prepared for the road ahead and whatever twists and turns it might bring. These principles are designed to help you realize your power, seize control of your future, and command respect and recognition for you. Just as I did by embracing these lessons, you have the potential to own your career journey and create the professional life of your dreams.

In the pages of this book, we've embarked on a transformative journey together. We've explored the depths of the administrative professional world, uncovering the profound transformation that comes from personal growth and professional development. As we bring this book to a close, my hope is that you take these principles and revelations to heart and apply them with the same passion and vigor that I did and continue to do.

May you find your own voice, may you carve your own path, and may you, too, experience the incredible fulfillment and empowerment that comes with being an Evolved Assistant. The journey doesn't end here; it's just the beginning of a brighter, more empowered future that you now hold the keys to unlock.

Acknowledgments

I want to express my heartfelt appreciation to all the incredible **administrative professionals** I've had the privilege of knowing, working closely with, mentoring, managing, and forming friendships with. This book couldn't exist without you. It's through all of you that I've gained valuable insights, shared stories, shared laughter, and even commiserated with about the frustrations we sometimes faced with challenging leaders, all of which have deepened my understanding of the collective and individual influence we possess in shaping countless organizations worldwide. My hope for us all is that as we continue to be support leaders, uplifting others in the background, helping to make our executives shine and organizations run more smoothly, and that we always take stock of our impact and recognize that wherever we are, our work matters!

I extend my deepest gratitude to the assistants who generously shared their stories for this book during our focus group sessions: **Jen Burns, Joanne Jennett, Nate Thaxton, Sally Lampi, Theresa Shultz,** and **Taylor Gillman.** Our time together was not only productive but also a whole lot of fun. You are truly among the best in the business.

To the **leaders** I've had the privilege of supporting directly or indirectly, I want to say thank you. Your leadership, expertise, words of support, and career guidance have been invaluable to me. I'm also grateful for those of you who challenged me to think bigger, differently, and helped me refine my skills, even when it didn't feel so great.

I can't forget to acknowledge the executives who have served as members of **my personal board of directors** (even though I probably never told you), expanding my perspective of the workplace and my role within it. I did not support many of you directly, yet you took an interest in me and always made time for me to "pick your brain." You know who you are.

A special shout-out goes to the thought leaders in the administrative field who continually champion our profession, nurture our community, and play an active role in my own professional development. **Maggie Jacobs, Debbie Gross, Bonnie Low-Kramen,** and **Jeremy Burrows,** your dedication is truly inspiring.

Mom (Rosalind Williams), thank you for being patient with me throughout this process. I know there were days when I was a bit grumpy, but you continued to be my biggest cheerleader and #1 fan. Oh, and you always made sure there was food in my stomach when I was working nights and weekends, not moving away from the computer for hours!

Daddy, (George Sims III), although you're not here with me, I feel your presence and often think about what you would have to say about some of my recent life experiences. I know you would be proud of me and of what I have been able to accomplish personally and professionally. Thank you for loving me. I miss you and our talks.

Aja Jackson, this project would not have been possible without your invaluable contributions. Your calm and steady presence kept me grounded throughout the process, especially when my nerves got the best of me. I can hear your soft voice, "You're almost there."

Jen Holloway, I can't thank you enough for being my go-to resource for all the random questions and challenges that came up during this project. Your knowledge has been a tremendous asset.

Adrienne Greaves, you have been my work guardian angel, advocating for me even when I wasn't in the room. Thank you for your continued support. Everyone needs someone like you.

Darnell McAlpin, your creative energy, and ability to bring my ideas to life are nothing short of genius. I swear you were a middle-aged woman in a past life because you can certainly put on your WWTD (What Would Tara Do) hat and show out! You've become the creative partner I never knew I needed. And congratulations on your first published book cover art! You understood the assignment.

Shawna Cohen, my dearest friend, and confidante, thank you for being the rational voice in my life, my brain when mine isn't working, saying yes to all the countless things I ask for including being held hostage to hear me read this book out loud, and who could forget the incessant laughing we do when we are together. That laughter is always healing to my soul. I cherish our friendship. Now cue the shenanigans in the background!

To the A Team: **Anittra Williams, Kisha Ward, Sherriah Johnson,** and **Joanne Jennett** – more than friends, you are my sisters. Your conversations, words of encouragement, and prayers always keep me going.

Bill Connors, thank you for allowing me to show up to work every day and be my authentic self. Everyone does not experience that with their manager, and it has been an incredible journey. Working with you has felt like a judgment-free zone, a rare gem in the workplace. Your leadership and friendship are priceless to me. You're the best, Big Guy, and you're stuck with me for life!

Resources

BOOKS FOR ADMINISTRATIVE PROFESSIONALS

(All can be found on Amazon)

The New Executive Assistant: Advice for Succeeding in Your Career by Melba Duncan (1997)

Building a Partnership with Your Boss (Take-Charge Assistant S) by Jerry Wisinski (1999)

The Definitive Executive Assistant and Managerial Handbook: A Professional Guide to Leadership for all PAs, Senior Secretaries, Office Managers and Executive Assistants by Sue France (2012)

Be the Ultimate Assistant: A Celebrity Assistant's Secret to Working with any High-Powered Employer by Bonnie Low-Kramen (2012)

Not "Just An Admin" by Peggy Vasquez (2014)

The CEO's Secret Weapon: How Great Leaders and Their Assistants Maximize Productivity and Effectiveness by Jan Jones (2015)

Jewel in the LEADER's CROWN: Powerful Strategies to Shine as an Executive Assistant & Beyond by Ruth Mead (2015)

Become A Procedures Pro: The Admin's Guide to Developing Effective Office Systems and Procedures by Julie Perrine (2017)

The New Executive Assistant: Exceptional Executive Office Management by Jonathan McIlroy (2018)

The Office Rockstar Playbook: How I Leveled Up as an Executive Assistant and Helped My CEO Build a Multibillion-Dollar Company by Debbie Gross (2019)

The Founder & Force Multiplier: How Entrepreneurs & Executive Assistants Achieve More Together by Adam Hergenrother & Hallie Warner (2019)

The Leader Assistant: Four Pillars of a Confident, Game-Changing Assistant by Jeremy Burrows (2020)

The Elevated EA: Find Your Voice & Own Your Future as an Executive Assistant by Maggie Jacobs (2020)

Elevate Admins: How to Raise the Bar and Achieve Excellence in Your Administrative Career by Chrissy Scivicque (2021)

The Modern-Day Assistant: Build Your Influence and Boost Your Potential by Lucy Brazier (2023)

PODCASTS FOR ADMINISTRATIVE PROFESSIONALS

Be the Ultimate Assistant Podcast (Launched 2015)

Assist With Impact with Liz Van Vliet (Launched 2016)

The Leader Assistant Podcast (Launched 2019)

Exceptional Admins (Launched 2019)

The Assistants Together Podcast (Launched 2019)

REACH – A Podcast for Executive Assistants (Launched 2019)

The Assistant Room (Launched 2019)

The EA Campus Podcast (Launched 2022)

References

1. **Harvard Business Review**. "How Has the Past Year Changed You and Your Organization?" *Harvard Business Review*, March 2021. https://hbr.org/2021/03/how-has-the-past-year-changed-you-and-your-organization.

2. Newport, Cal. *So Good They Can't Ignore You: Why Skills Trump Passion in the Quest for Work You Love.* New York: Grand Central Publishing, 2012.

3. Dweck, Carol S. *Mindset: The New Psychology of Success.* New York: Ballantine Books, 2006.

4. Duarte, Nancy. *Slideology: The Art and Science of Creating Great Presentations.* Sebastopol, CA: O'Reilly Media, 2008.

5. Dweck, Carol S. *Mindset: The New Psychology of Success.* New York: Ballantine Books, 2006.

6. *The Untethered Soul: The Journey Beyond Yourself.* Singer, Michael A. Oakland, CA: New Harbinger Publications, 2007.

About the author

Tara M. Sims is an award-winning administrative leader, executive support expert, and owner of Evolved Assistant, a boutique virtual assistant agency. Born in New Orleans and now based in Atlanta, Tara is passionate about fostering the success of corporate executives, business owners, and the administrative professionals who support them. With a Bachelor of Arts degree in Psychology from Denison University, Tara's career began in college recruitment, where she served as Assistant Director of Admissions. Over a successful 20-year career, she has evolved into a dynamic, strategic problem solver and executive partner, supporting C-suite leaders and senior-level professionals within Fortune 500 companies. Her expertise spans traditional administrative functions, administrative leadership, team building, and coaching. Tara's proven ability to adapt to changing business needs, workplace cultures, and executive personalities makes her an asset in building successful, collaborative relationships.

Nominated by executives and recognized by her peers, Tara received the 2021 Admin Awards Leadership Award. She has also been a featured guest on The Leader Assistant Podcast, The EA Campus Podcast, and at the World 50 Executive Administration Program.

When not fostering business success, she enjoys HIIT workouts, exploring Georgia's scenic trails, traveling, and sharing great meals with family and friends. Additionally, Tara is a licensed cosmetologist, a member of Alpha Kappa Alpha Sorority, Inc., and a member of the Speakers Bureau for the Foundation for Sarcoidosis Research.

Visit https://www.evolvedassistant.com/ for more information.

Made in the USA
Columbia, SC
05 December 2024